How to Have
the Mind of Christ

An Introduction to Biblical Coaching

Lesley Malpas

New Wine Press

New Wine Ministries
PO Box 17
Chichester
West Sussex
United Kingdom
PO19 2AW

ISBN 978-1-905991-18-1

Typeset by CRB Associates, Reepham, Norfolk
Cover design by CCD, www.ccdgroup.co.uk
Author photo by Claude Malpas
Printed in Malta

Contents

Dedication

For Alex, Oliver, Sam and Josh, my absolutely amazing sons.
Thank you for your unwavering love and support.
To my wonderful friends, especially Charlotte and Emma,
for all your encouragement and faith through the dark moments.
And to my husband, Anthony, for surrounding me
with never-ending love, patience and prayer!

Introduction

It will not surprise you to read that many people on earth today live in utterly desperate situations. You may not, however, be aware that equally there are many in the Body of Christ who also live without any hope or vision for their lives, often doubting God's Word and His ability to answer prayer. Thousands of believers are suffering from depression and some are in such utter despair that they have reached the point of attempting to commit suicide.

Behind all of these situations is the work of a very real spiritual being and in this book you will discover how he works undetected in the minds even of the children of God. But our Saviour, Jesus Christ, came to destroy the works of the devil (1 John 3:8) and to bring vision and hope, healing and deliverance to people on earth (Luke 4:18). Today He is using biblical coaching to destroy the work of evil in people's lives and to release them from oppression through the power of the Holy Spirit and the authority of the Word of God.

As the Lord's Body on earth we must learn how to overcome the enemy through the renewing of our minds, because this is the place where the spiritual battle for our lives and the lives of every human being alive is fought out. I daily witness the Lord drive out oppression and restore people's lives as they learn how to renew their minds and He is raising up this ministry firstly to bring healing to us as His children, and then to bring healing and deliverance to the people all around us. We must become strong in the Word of God and overcome the enemy (1 John 2:14) in order to truly help people, because according to the Scriptures, the problems in people's lives are caused and masterminded by spiritual forces of darkness (Ephesians 6). As believers we are the only ones who have the authority and power of Jesus on earth over this darkness.

This book is written to bring teaching and understanding to the Body of Christ about the critical importance for a believer of the renewing of the mind, to establish the ministry, principles and practices of biblical coaching, to provide a handbook for believers who want to train and become biblical coaches, and to minister healing and deliverance to both those in the Body and outside who are in desperate or difficult circumstances in their lives.

Biblical coaching

Biblical coaching is founded only on the Word of God and operates in and through the leading of the Spirit of God. It is a ministry of the Holy Spirit to continue the work of the Lord Jesus to bind up the broken hearted, to proclaim freedom for the captives, and release for the prisoners from the darkness – all of which takes place first and foremost in the mind (Luke 4:18).

At the core of biblical coaching is the process of renewing your mind with the Word of God in order that the old nature and the old belief system is removed, and the new nature, the new belief system of the mind of Jesus Christ, is put on. This process forms His very nature in you and therefore the power of His life can be released through you more and more as your mind continues to be renewed. The biblical coaching process identifies the activity of the old nature in your life, and shows that behind the old nature is the work of the enemy of your soul, the devil.

In this book you will discover how Satan attacks and interferes with your mind to prevent you from realising your full God-given call and potential, and you will learn how to be set free and to remove his influence from your life. This will and can only happen through your partnership with the Spirit of God, and by His power. You will learn how to become free from the darkness that can destroy your walk with God, and how to be released into your true potential, which is to fulfil the purpose for which God created you to live on this earth.

The difference between biblical coaching and secular coaching

The rapidly growing profession of secular Life Coaching started with the work of one man, Professor Timothy Gallwey of Harvard University. From his studies of the game of tennis he made a discovery that was to change sports psychology for ever. Professor Gallwey created the equation: "performance equals potential minus interference" and concluded that a tennis match was won first and foremost in the player's mind. The obstacles that hindered a player's performance could be removed through the coaching process that he had developed. Gallwey went on to apply the truth of his findings to the business world and finally the concepts were applied to secular life and hence the profession of life coaching was born. What Professor Gallwey actually discovered were biblical principles that are recorded over and over in the Scriptures, for example, *"As he* [a man] *thinks in his heart, so is he"* (Proverbs 23:7).

Secular life coaching does help many people to turn their lives around, but coaching without the Spirit of God cannot bring lasting deliverance and change because the problems in people's lives are masterminded by a spiritual being, the devil (see Ephesians 6). True deliverance and lasting change can only be experienced through faith in the Lord Jesus Christ.

Biblical coaching applies the eternal victory of Jesus to people's lives. Secular coaching cannot do that.

Biblical coaching operates at a very different level, in a different dimension from secular coaching. By working under the leading of the Spirit of God it is possible to identify the hidden work of the enemy that lies at the root of the problem. Secular coaching only deals with the symptoms of the problem as it presents itself. By identifying the interference of the enemy in people's lives and teaching them how to be set free from oppression by the power of the Spirit, through the renewing of their minds, they are delivered and permanently set free to fulfil the vision and destiny that God has purposed for their lives.

Biblical coaching is totally centred on Jesus, His victory and His redemptive plan for your life. Secular coaching is focused on the individual and the individual's plan for their life. In secular coaching there is the coach and the coachee; in biblical coaching there is the Holy Spirit, the biblical coach ministering under the anointing and leading of the Spirit, and the coachee.

Today

The Lord has used the truths that I share in this book to restore my own life and His redemptive plan is unfolding more and more as I continue to apply the principles I have learned from Him. In the lives of those I have had the privilege to coach I have seen people on the verge of suicide instantly given hope and their lives totally turned around in a period of weeks. Depression is a spiritual problem and millions of believers are suffering in the Body today because they have not known who is behind the suicidal, self-harming thoughts that they have battled with. I have seen obsessive disorders broken, marriages on the verge of divorce turned around, hope restored, and lives rebuilt through the wonderful and powerful work of the Holy Spirit in people's minds.

My experience with the Lord in this ministry has shown me that He loves biblical coaching because it opens the door for Him to work at the heart of the problem in people's lives, in their belief systems. My prayer for you is that you, and through you others who you know, will be released from limiting beliefs about God and about yourself through the words of truth on the pages of this book. There is no pit too deep, no sin too great, and no problem so large that cannot be reached, cleansed or solved by the power of the risen Lord Jesus. With Him anything is possible and I pray that the Lord will open your mind now to receive truth and power from Him which will really transform your life.

The Invisible Substance of Life

"By faith we understand that the worlds were framed by the word of God, so that the things which are seen were not made of things which are visible." (Hebrews 11:3)

Do you know that the original DNA of everything that you see around you in the natural world was created by nothing other than the spoken word of God? And do you know that He hasn't changed; that when God wants to create life today, He speaks? Do you know that He created you in His exact likeness and with the ability to release His creative power through your spoken words? Do you know the incredible implication this has for you?

In Hebrews 11:3 we read that God created the universe, the things that are now seen, out of things that were unseen; His word. However, before God speaks He thinks, and His words are none other than the revelation to us of the thoughts and desires of the invisible world of His heart. His words are the containers, which carry His power to create His desires; God's words are the invisible substance of His life. But are you aware that your words reveal the thoughts and desires of your heart, and that your words are containers that carry the power that shapes your life and determines your destiny? Do you know that your words are the invisible substance of your life? Your spoken words are meant to be the vehicles that carry the power of God to bring forth His will and purposes for your life on earth.

Created in His image

> *"Then God said, 'Let Us make man in Our image, according to our likeness' . . . So God created man in His own image; in the image of God He created him; male and female He created them."*
>
> (Genesis 1:26–27)

When God created Adam, He created him with a deep love; He created him to succeed, not to fail, to be a blessing, not a curse. God created Adam to rule on earth. You were in the heart of the Father on the day that Adam was created, and when He shaped the first man in His image and placed in him His attributes and power, Father God was shaping and creating you. You are created in His exact likeness and you are created to rule, to succeed and to be a blessing on the earth.

Freewill

The most amazing gift of love, that God placed within Adam on the day of creation, and therefore in you, was the gift of freewill. Freewill gives you total freedom, in your internal world, to choose what you think, what you say and therefore how you act in any situation. When God gave you freewill, He gave you power, and with this power personal responsibility for your life. Freewill is essential for freedom, because if no one can control your inner thought life and your spoken words, then ultimately they cannot control you or your destiny. And if you are a believer in the Lord Jesus this means that there is absolutely no situation in your life, no aspect of your personality, and no circumstance that cannot be changed through your faith in Him.

The start of the rebellion

Imagine the moment; Adam, fully aware that he is about to break the commandment he had directly received from the Father, and yet he is totally blind to the terrible and serious consequences that a single act of rebellion would bring into effect for himself, for Eve, for their offspring, and for all who would be born into this world, for you and for me. He takes that first bite into the forbidden fruit of the Tree of the Knowledge of Good and Evil, and the deed is done.

With immediate effect the right to rule on earth was transferred from Adam to Satan; this fallen angel had become the god of the earth, for this age, and had stolen our birthright through his greatest of skills, deception. But there is a question to be answered; on the day that Adam fell, did Satan also take absolute power to rule and control the lives and destinies of every man and woman who was to be born into this world? The answer is no, because of the internal gift of freewill. Fallen man still retained and held on to the gift and the right to freedom of choice; fallen man was still created in God's image and still retained His attributes.

Man still had internal freedom to choose life or death, to choose to follow Satan or the Father God who had created him. We see this beginning immediately with the life of Abel through to Enoch, Noah, Abraham, Joseph, Moses, Samuel and David, to name but a few of the Old Testament saints. These men chose to follow God through the power of freewill, still at work within them. They retained the ability to shape their lives and control their destiny, and so do you. God gave you a gift that would provide you with a way back to Him, freedom to choose, to choose Him through faith in the One who would come and pay the price for the redemption of the human race, His Son, the Lord Jesus Christ.

Who holds the keys to your future?

Every man and woman on earth today is descended from
Adam and is therefore born in a fallen state. However, each
human being still retains the ability to shape his or her life,
because man's will is still free; you are free to choose how you
will live your life. Because of freewill you hold the keys to
your future and therefore you are the one who will ultimately
determine where you end up in life! God has a plan and a
purpose for you, but the power of freewill leaves you totally
free to choose whether or not you will engage with Him
and fulfil your God-given destiny, or turn away from Him and
continue to go your own way. Your future, even as a believer,
is not a forgone conclusion.

The fact that God has given you responsibility for your life is
wonderful news, because this means that He has placed within
you everything you need to bring about the change you
require, right now! As you learn how to harness freewill, by
choosing life through the Spirit of God, the power of God will
be made available to you in your inner man. And for a child of
God, led by the Spirit of God, who knows how to operate this
internal system through faith as God intended, there is no one
and no situation that can ultimately hold you down.

The invisible world of the inner man

Your inner man resides within you, this is your internal world,
it is who you really are; it is the invisible, hidden side of your
life, your thought life, your personal beliefs, your values, the
memories and the experiences that have shaped you and
made you who you are today; this is your inner man.

The inner man is made up of your soul and your spirit. It is
your core, your centre, your heart. The inner man was
created to commune with God and through Him to create
your outer physical world. This is the part of you that is

responsible for driving and shaping your life; this is where God Himself dwells and works within you.

God created you to be a visionary. He created you with a mind that is able to see and envision that which as yet does not exist, so that you can bring forth His will and purposes on the earth through this inner vision and through your spoken words; all men inherently have this ability from God. The account of the tower of Babel shows us that when men are of one mind, united around a common goal, and when they are verbally in agreement then whatever they plan can be accomplished:

> *"And the LORD said, 'Indeed the people are one and they all have one language, and this is what they begin to do; now nothing that they propose to do will be withheld from them.'"*   (Genesis 11:6)

The word "propose" in this text is translated from the Hebrew word *zamam*, which means "to meditate, to think, to consider, to plot, to purpose", which are all activities of the mind. It is used numerous times in the Old Testament to refer to the plans of the Lord and the plans of men:

> *"'Just as I **determined** [zamam] to punish you*
> *When your fathers provoked Me to wrath,'*
> *Says the LORD of Hosts,*
> *'And I would not relent,*
> *So again in these days*
> *I am **determined** to do good*
> *To Jerusalem and to the house of Judah.*
> *Do not fear.'"*   (Zechariah 8:14–15, emphasis added)

The same word is used in Proverbs 31 in the description of the characteristics and activities of a virtuous wife:

> *"She **considers** [zamam] a field and buys it;*
> *From her profits she plants a vineyard."*
>
>   (Proverbs 31:16, emphasis added)

Here we see that the virtuous wife not only had a plan to buy a field, but she also had a vision to develop the field, she imagined it planted with vines, and in due time through the profits from her other activities she then acts on the vision and the vineyard is planted.

However, from the beginning Satan has used man's ability to plan and envision the future to bring about his own evil purposes. And the terrible revelation is that if you are not serving God Almighty with all your mind then you are serving the god of this world, Satan himself; it is black and white, no grey areas here. Today Satan is still stealing, twisting and using man's authority on earth for his own purposes, namely to seek to destroy mankind: *"the thief does not come except to steal, and to kill, and to destroy"* (John 10:10).

We see this at its worst ultimately and supremely displayed in the lives of men filled with evil such as Rudolf Hoess, the commandant of Auschwitz concentration camp. His mind, satanically inspired, devised the techniques of mass murder which would allow the Nazis to implement the Final Solution. These were first conceived and envisioned in his mind and then they became an awful reality. The events of 9/11 were all conceived in the minds of men; every atrocity you can think of starts with the seed of a thought in the mind. This is the terrible potential that inherently resides within every human being: *"an evil man out of the evil treasure of his heart brings forth evil"* (Luke 6:45).

Daily, men and women shape their own lives without the knowledge of God through this divinely given creative ability, and a glance at any newspaper reveals the chaos and destruction at work in the world today through man's misuse and the enemy's use of this power. God created the human mind with the ability to plan and see the future. This ability empowers men to shape their lives and therefore ultimately decide their eternal destiny; it is the decisions that you make every day that determine where you will end up in life. The greatest tragedy for a man or woman is to reach the end of their life on earth and suddenly come to the revelation that it was their own thoughts that led them to make the choice to reject the salvation and promise of eternal life through Jesus Christ. Such is the power of your thought life; truly it can lead you to life or death.

The Kingdom of Heaven

As a believer in Jesus Christ you have been transferred into another kingdom and so into another dimension, another realm, and you now have the awesome power of the Spirit of God dwelling within you. He wants to work through your mind, through your thoughts, through your inner man to create the life that the Father ordained for you before the foundation of the world. He wants to work salvation and redemption through you; He wants to work with you to shape your visible, physical world from within. But how, how do you work with the Spirit to create and shape your life from within? To answer this we need to understand what the Word of God tells us about the dwelling place of the Spirit, where He lives, how He works within a man, how we grieve Him, how we obey Him, and how we access and live in the victory He has won for us.

In Galatians 4:6 we read:

> *"And because you are sons, God has sent forth the Spirit of His Son into your hearts, crying out, 'Abba, Father!' "*

The Spirit of the Lord Jesus Christ resides in your heart. What exactly does this mean?

There are hundreds of references in the Bible relating to the heart, but what is the Holy Spirit referring to? Is He speaking about the physical heart beating within you, or is He using figurative imagery to relate to something else? The original

Hebrew and Greek translation of the Scriptures show that the word translated "heart" in the Bible is not referring to your physical heart, it is referring to the heart of you, the centre of your being; the Holy Spirit is speaking about your inner man. In biblical language your heart, your inner man, is your mind, conscious and subconscious, and all the various activities it performs, and it is here, through the work of the cross, that the Spirit of the Son of God Himself has taken up residence; the Lord Jesus Christ operates in the control centre of your entire being, in your mind.

CHAPTER 2

In the Beginning...

In the Old Testament the word "heart" is translated from the Hebrew word *leb* and refers to the heart as the middle, the centre of something. *Leb* is used to describe the inner man and the mind. First Corinthians 10:6 tells us that we are meant to learn from Israel's history: *"Now these things occurred as examples to keep us from setting our hearts on evil things"* (NIV). The Scriptures are there to teach us; we are to learn from them, so what can we learn about the human mind from the Old Covenant?

As we read the accounts of the men and women in the Old Covenant we constantly see three forces at work, the Spirit of God operating in the human mind, the power of the human mind itself, and the work of the enemy in the minds of men. All through the Old Covenant the battlefield is the human mind.

The Lord's work with mankind on earth began in the Garden of Eden, and it is here we see these three forces in action. The account of the events in the Garden of Eden reveals the battle tactics of the enemy of man, Satan, and how he attacked Adam and Eve in their minds; his same strategy has been played out on earth against human beings ever since. The Son of God Himself was subject to the very same attack as Adam and Eve, but He did not fail. Why is this relevant to you? Because the attack is directly aimed at your mind and specifically your belief system, and, as you will discover, the struggles you are facing today can only be won in this same arena – the mind.

When God gave Adam the command not to eat of the tree of the Knowledge of Good and Evil, the Word of God went into Adam's brain. It went from his conscious into his subconscious, and was intended to build a belief system which would guide his thought life and steer his actions. Adam was free to choose to obey or to rebel against his Creator's words; this decision-making process is an activity of the conscious mind. A study of the events of the Garden of Eden tells us that only Eve was deceived, which means that Adam was fully conscious that his actions were against the commandment he had received from the Lord. So let us now look at the strategy of Satan more closely.

Genesis 2:25 describes the state of Adam and Eve before Satan's attack on their minds: *". . . and they were both naked, the man and his wife, and were **not** ashamed"* (emphasis added). The word translated "ashamed", comes from the Hebrew *bos* meaning "ashamed, disgraced, humiliated". *Bos* denotes shattered human emotions, confusion, dismay, embarrassment, disillusionment and a broken spirit. All of these words relate to the thought life and emotions that people now commonly experience, but *Adam and Eve did not have any of these negative beliefs and emotions before the fall*. This verse lays the foundation for the fundamental mental change that was about to take place in these two people, a change that was to have a profound effect on the minds and lives of every person who has ever lived, apart from Jesus Christ Himself.

We then read in chapter 3 of Satan's conversation with Eve. He did not actually speak to Adam, but as we see in verse 6, Adam was with Eve, listening to the conversation and fully aware of what was happening.

Satan's attack came into Eve's mind in three ways: distortion, doubt and deception, and these three are all targeted at the belief system. All words are seeds and the first seeds Satan sowed were words designed to create distortion. *"Has God indeed said, 'You shall not eat of every tree of the garden?'"* (Genesis 3:1). In his opening sentence he purposely distorts the commandment of God. Eve replies, *"We may eat the fruit of the trees of the garden; but of the fruit of the tree which is in the midst of the garden, God has said, 'You shall not eat it, nor shall you touch it, lest you die'"* (Genesis 3:2–3). It is clear that Eve understood the commandment even though she had added to it, as God did not say that it could not be touched.

Having subtly introduced distortion, Satan now develops his strategy; he knows the commandment that God has given to Adam and he has a clear objective in his mind, which, through the words he speaks, is to get Adam and Eve to break the commandment by eating the fruit of the tree of the Knowledge of Good and Evil. He now makes a tactical move; he sows the seeds of doubt and deception.

> *"You will not surely die. For God knows that in the day you eat of it your eyes will be opened, and you will be like God, knowing good and evil."* (Genesis 3:4–5)

These words are created for one purpose – to divide Eve's mind, to create that second thought, to generate unbelief, and to gain access to her "heart", her mind. And he succeeds. Eve's belief system changes, she doubts God's word, she is now focused on Satan's word and on the promise of becoming like God, and she is deceived into believing that the outcome will be good and that the fruit will bring her wisdom. She is already thinking in a different way through the introduction of a different kind of knowledge that has come directly from Satan's words.

> *"When the woman saw that the tree was good for food, that it was*
> *pleasant to the eyes, and a tree desirable to make one wise, she took*
> *of its fruit and ate."*   (Genesis 3:6)

The word for "saw" here is *ra'ah* in the Hebrew, meaning "to understand intellectually, to perceive, to discover". Eve was intellectually deceived; her understanding had changed. She had physically seen the fruit before but until this point Eve had the Word of God in her mind and had kept His commandment.

> The words of Satan changed her belief and therefore her
> perception; it is at this point that she transgressed,
> and then she acted on her new belief.

Eve was deceived through the process of distortion, doubt and deception. Adam was not deceived, but he also ate the fruit.

> *"And Adam was not deceived, but the woman being deceived, fell*
> *into transgression."*   (1 Timothy 2:14)

When Adam took the fruit out of Eve's hand and ate, he absolutely knew he was breaking the command of God. He made a freewill decision to operate outside the Word of God and the second he made that decision he committed sin; his mind had become divided; his actions were purely the manifestation of the change that had already taken place in his belief system. He had stopped serving the Lord with all his heart.

The immediate result of their now defiled and divided minds, one through deception the other through an act of disobedience and rebellion, was that their eyes were opened and they knew that they were naked. For the first time, in their minds, they began to experience *bos*, shame, disgrace, humiliation, shattered human emotions, confusion, dismay, embarrassment, disillusionment and a broken spirit. And then, as never before, a new sensation entered the human mind; they experienced fear.

Jesus taught in Matthew 5:21–30 that sin takes place in the mind first and in fact that sin is actually committed in the mind. Satan knew this; it had been his own experience and his aim was to lead Adam into temptation and Eve into deception through their thoughts, because once the act is committed in the mind, from God's point of view, you are defiled. The fall of Adam and Eve took place in their minds, and every fall of every human being takes place in the mind through this very same format and with the same influence, the influence of Satan.

So why does Satan desire to destroy human beings in this way? Because this is exactly what happened to him; he operated outside the commandment of God and became divided and defiled, and was cast out of God's presence. His rebellion and defilement turned him into a liar and a murderer (John 8:44); he is *the* original sinner according to 1 John 3:8, *"the devil has sinned from the beginning"*. His aim in the Garden was to turn man into his likeness by defiling him in the same way that he had defiled himself; and this is exactly what he achieved.

Adam and Eve committed sin in their minds through choosing to operate in a knowledge that was different from the knowledge they had received from God; they chose to operate in the fallen sinful knowledge that came from Satan. There was no sin until Satan was in their presence; he was the first of God's creation to sin and he is the one who leads all men in to sin.

By eating the fruit of the tree of the Knowledge of Good and Evil, with minds that had become defiled, Adam and Eve received a kind of knowledge and wisdom that they did not have before. For us to overcome and live victorious lives as believers, we need to understand the difference between the knowledge and wisdom of this world, which is from Satan, and the knowledge and wisdom of God.

At the end of his letter to the Romans, 16:19–20, Paul makes a direct reference to the events in the Garden of Eden, and provides us, as believers in Jesus, with the antidote to what took place in the minds of Adam and Eve:

> *"Everyone has heard about your obedience, so I am full of joy over you; but I want you to be wise about what is good, and innocent about what is evil. The God of peace will soon crush Satan under your feet."*   (NIV)

There are two key words here: "wise" and "innocent". The Greek word for "wise" is *sophos* and in biblical terms this means the wisdom of God, not man, the wisdom that is from above, not the wisdom of the world, which James tells us is evil, James 3:15 says, *"This wisdom does not descend from above, but is earthly, sensual, demonic."* *Sophos* denotes a knowledge and understanding of God's ways and the ability to apply that knowledge practically. In this verse Paul is appealing for us to have understanding and knowledge of what God terms and reveals to be good, and to have His wisdom to practise and apply that goodness in His way through righteous acts. This is very different from the wisdom of the world which is under the power of Satan.

The Greek word for "innocent" is *akeraios*, meaning "unmixed, unamalgamated, unblended", and relates to the ethical character, the morals, the belief system and the thoughts of a person. So in regard to evil we are not to be mixed, blended or amalgamated in any way; this is what it means to be innocent or simple concerning evil. We are not to entertain any evil thoughts, we are not to have knowledge of evil but rather set our minds on,

"... whatever things are true, whatever things are noble, whatever things are just, whatever things are pure, whatever things are lovely, whatever things are of good report, if there is any virtue and if there is anything praiseworthy – meditate on these things."

(Philippians 4:8)

Biblical positive thinking is not optional,
it is essential if you are to resist evil in your mind.

Let us return to the Garden of Eden now and compare the scripture in Romans 16:19–20 with what the Lord spoke to Satan after the fall in Genesis 3:15:

"And I will put enmity
  between you and the woman,
  and between your offspring and hers;
he will crush your head,
  and you will strike at his heel."   (NIV)

Why does the Lord promise to crush Satan's head? The head contains the brain, the brain contains the knowledge and the wisdom and it is the presence of this evil knowledge and wisdom that works in the old nature. For this reason the old belief system, mindset and nature must be cut out, put off, crushed and crucified. All of this happens through belief, through faith and through the renewing of your mind. The Lord Jesus has already crushed and destroyed the power of Satan, but each one of us must personally receive this victory by faith. You experience His victory in your life through the active process of renewing your mind. It is a renewed mind full of faith and free from doubt and unbelief that causes the victory of the Lord Jesus to become increasingly manifest in your life.

In order to experience this promise, firstly you must receive the knowledge of God from the Spirit of God and the Word of God, which is the absolute opposite to operating in the wisdom of the world, and secondly, you must totally cast out and reject evil thoughts, which is the pulling down of strongholds, beliefs and any knowledge which contradicts the Word of God.

What we have seen in this chapter is that the fall of Adam and Eve occurred in their minds, their conscious and unconscious thoughts and beliefs, and that they acquired a type of knowledge and wisdom that was absolutely contrary to the Word of God. We have learned that this came directly from Satan, and that his aim and desire is to influence men and women away from God by causing them to have divided minds that lead to deception and unbelief. We have also seen that God gave every man the precious gift of freewill, so that everyone who has ever lived has a choice to make, whether to listen to the lies of Satan or the truth of God's Word.

We are now going to look at the consequences of the fall in the hearts and minds of people who lived before Jesus came to bring salvation and the power to crush Satan under our feet.

The Kings of Israel and Judah

Over and over again we see in the Old Covenant writings that the state of a king's heart, that is his mindset, determined his relationship with God. The kings of Judah swung like a pendulum between good and evil. When a king *"served the LORD with his whole heart"* according to the command of Deuteronomy 6:5, the kingdom prospered and was blessed and protected by God; the enemy was shut out. And again without exception, whenever a king *"did evil"* in the sight of the Lord, it was always because his heart, his mind, had turned away from God. Success or failure, life or death, blessing or curse for the nation was wrapped up in the condition of the heart of the king; it all came down to the state of his mind.

Satan knew that if he could get into the king's thought life and divide his mind against the Lord, then he could lead him into idolatry and every evil practice. So who would the king follow? What would he choose? He had freewill and the power to choose life or death, blessing or curse, the word of the Lord or the word of the devil; the Garden of Eden was relived every day.

David and Solomon

David was a man who understood the power of his mind. He understood the mind and the ways of the Lord and actively pursued Him throughout his whole life. He knew how to focus his mind wholly on God, and that is absolutely the reason why he had such intimacy with the Lord. Even in his darkest moments, and in the times of his life when he turned away and momentarily experienced division in his mind, he came running back to the Lord with all that he was, and it was this wholehearted, undivided mental capacity and love for the Lord that attracted the strong presence of God in his life.

When David fell into sin he didn't stay there, he got up and he went on with the Lord. He could do this because he understood God's deep covenant love for him and God's mercy to those who turn from sin. David is an example to us of how to mentally handle a fall in our lives. He learnt from his personal experiences, he drew knowledge and wisdom from the dark times in his life, and he taught his son Solomon all he knew about following the Lord; specifically he warned him about the perils of not following God wholeheartedly, having identified this as the reason for his own fall.

David taught Solomon that wisdom was the principal thing, so that when the Lord appeared to Solomon at Gibeon in 1 Kings 3:5 he acted on his father's words and asked the Lord not for riches, not for long life, but for wisdom, God's wisdom. The Scriptures go on to record that God answered this request and gave Solomon largeness of heart, which was a huge mental capacity of understanding; it was Solomon's brain that God touched and, apart from the Son of God Himself, Solomon was the wisest man that ever lived. So what on earth caused him to turn away from the Lord at the end of his life?

Satanic assignment

> *"For it was so, when Solomon was old, that his wives turned his heart after other gods; and his heart was not loyal to the LORD his God, as was the heart of his father David."*   (1 Kings 11:4)

In 1 Kings 11:2 we read the commandment that God specifically repeated to Solomon:

"You shall not intermarry with them, nor they with you. Surely they will turn away your hearts after their gods."

The Lord knew Solomon's weakness, and with these words He was warning Solomon of a future demonic assignment on his life, but Solomon missed what the Spirit was saying; he missed the opportunity to renew his mind and prepare himself for Satan's attack. And so the distraction came, and Solomon's mind was captured, the enemy had found a way in, the mind of the king of Israel was now divided, and full devotion to the Lord his God was gone. The result was catastrophic; he ended up worshipping the demons of pagan gods.

"For Solomon went after Ashtoreth the goddess of the Sidonians, and after Milcom the abomination of the Amonites . . . So the LORD became angry with Solomon, because his heart had turned away from the LORD God of Israel, who had appeared to him twice, and had commanded him concerning this thing, that he should not go after other gods, but he did not keep what the LORD had commanded." (1 Kings 11:5, 9–10)

Here is the second greatest and wisest man that ever lived. How tragic that at the end of his life he ended up doing evil in the sight of the Lord. Why? It was because of the state of his mind; it was Solomon's mind that became divided and consequently his belief system changed and ultimately he acted against the will of God.

Solomon is a great Old Covenant example to us of just how critical it is to guard our minds. We must stick to God's Word, listen, and act on the promptings and warnings of the Holy Spirit every day of our lives. We do this by renewing our minds with His truth. In the Old Covenant the renewing of the mind was described as the circumcision of the heart, and just as with physical circumcision, renewing the mind is not automatic, it is a proactive work that we must undertake and perform with the Spirit.

Solomon saw the most amazing manifestation of the glory of God during his reign as king. However, this did not protect him from the devil's assignment on his life. It is not the anointing that protects you; you can be anointed and be in deception. It is awareness of how your enemy works, obedience to the Word of God and a mindset totally after the Spirit that brings protection.

A divided mind is so dangerous; firstly it separates you from the fullness of the Lord's presence, His power and His blessing, because a divided mind operates in doubt and unbelief. And secondly, the writer of the Epistle to the Hebrews tells us that an unbelieving heart is evil, because it opens a door for the devil and his aim is to lead you further and further away from the Lord and ultimately on a road to disaster; the end of Solomon's life teaches us this.

The devil wants to take the place of God in your mind; he wants your worship and undivided attention and he uses the things of this world to get it. If he can put something or someone in your life that can either take first place in your mind, or cause you to doubt the Lord and His Word, then he has divided your mind and has an in-road into your life, and he will use it over and over again until you are in bondage to him. He knows you can't serve God with a divided mind and so his goal is to create circumstances and events that are specifically aimed at distracting and attracting you with one aim, to create a stronghold in your belief system.

Josiah

*"Now before him there was no king like him, who turned to the LORD with **all** his heart, with all his soul, and with all his might,*

*according to all the Law of Moses; nor after him did any arise
like him."*   (2 Kings 23:25, emphasis added)

Every true act of repentance involves a change of mind, a
turning of the divided part of our minds back to God, which
results in a renewed passion for the Lord and His Word. Josiah
restored true worship when he set his mind to follow the Lord
and His Word with his whole being. When he read the book
of the covenant which was found in the temple, he was torn to
the heart; light entered his mind as the Word of God cut
through and convicted him; revelation by the Spirit instantly
changed his belief system. Immediately he took action and
made a covenant before the Lord to follow Him and keep His
commandments, His testimonies and His statutes with all of
his heart and all of his soul, with a totally united mind, and he
did it!

His full mental commitment to God that day affected the
entire nation and a process was set in motion to rid the people
completely of all idolatry, which is the fruit of a divided mind.
He rid the nation of evil practices and restored the Passover
once again in such a way as had never been done before by the
kings of Judah and Israel.

King Josiah was a man just like us, but he is an example of
an Old Covenant believer who actually did it; he loved God
with all his heart, no compromise. If it was possible for King
Josiah under the Old Covenant then it is more than possible
for you and me under the New Covenant; in fact it is the
Lord's deepest desire.

When it comes to the ministry of biblical coaching the aim of
the Holy Spirit is to set the mind of a man or woman free to
serve the Lord, by uncovering the hidden work of the enemy.
Satan has been working secretly, largely undetected, in the

minds of human beings since the fall of man, and it is for this reason that the Son of God has poured His Spirit into our minds, to evict, undo and destroy the enemy's work in each one of us. Your mind is the battleground, the Lord has made His home there and He wants to pull down every stronghold, and manifest His victory over Satan in your life through the renewing of your mind. He wants to restore your mind to an even greater state than Adam and Eve had before the fall, because through the renewing of your mind by the Word and the Spirit, the mind of Messiah is now being formed in you. *"But we have the mind of Christ"* (1 Corinthians 2:16).

This miraculous work is at the heart of the promise of the New Covenant given in Jeremiah. The Lord promised He would come and write His Torah on the minds of men by His Spirit coming to dwell within them; He would come to replace the old rotten, polluted and defiled mind with the pure spotless undefiled mind of Christ. But the gift of freewill means you are involved, firstly by calling on His name and receiving Jesus as your Lord and Saviour, the one decision that changed your life forever, and secondly by renewing your mind with His Word so that you develop a mindset after the Spirit. It is the failure of believers to renew their minds on a daily basis that leads to so much unhappiness, strife, despair, unanswered prayer, poverty, broken relationships, depression and in extreme cases attempted suicide. The promise of the Father through the work of the Spirit of God is to fully form the Son of God in you through the knowledge of Him.

This is the aim and purpose of the process of biblical coaching: to liberate you from the fallen mind of Adam, which is the old nature, and enable you to put on the new nature which is the pure, spotless mind of Jesus Christ.

The lesson from the Old Covenant that I know the Lord wants to draw out in this book, is that the enemy of your soul seeks to prevent you being transformed into the image of Jesus Christ and he does this by gaining access to your life through your old fallen belief system. Grasp this and you will start to identify how he is stealing from you today; use the biblical coaching skills in this book and the Holy Spirit will evict Satan, your mind will be renewed and the presence of the Lord will grow and grow in your life.

In the following scriptures the Hebrew word *leb* is translated as "heart" and in every instance this refers to the mind as a whole, the conscious and subconscious. Study these scriptures carefully and you will find how your mind has power to determine your destiny.

The heart of man in the Old Covenant

Your mind, is the place where wisdom and understanding reside

> "And God gave Solomon wisdom and exceedingly great understanding, and largeness of heart [capacity in the mind] like the sand on the seashore." (1 Kings 4:29)

Your mind, is the place where God places gifts, skills, ability

> "And He has put in his heart [mind] the ability to teach . . . He has filled them with skill to do all manner of work . . . "
> (Exodus 35:34–35)

Serving God with all your heart, with an undivided mind, will cause you to prosper

> "And in every work that he began in the service of the house of God, in the law and in the commandment, to seek his God, he did it with all his heart. So he prospered." (2 Chronicles 31:21)

Your state of mind affects your countenance and outer appearance

> "Therefore the king said to me, 'Why is your face sad, since you are not sick? This is nothing but sorrow of heart . . .' "
>
> (Nehemiah 2:2)

> "A merry heart makes a cheerful countenance,
> But by sorrow of the heart the spirit is broken."
>
> (Proverbs 15:13)

Your state of mind affects your physical body

> "A sound heart is life to the body,
> But envy is rottenness to the bones."   (Proverbs 14:30)

Your state of mind determines your mental health and wellbeing

> "Anxiety in the heart of man causes depression."
>
> (Proverbs 12:25)

> "Hope deferred makes the heart sick,
> But when desire comes, it is a tree of life."   (Proverbs 13:12)

> "A merry heart does good, like medicine."   (Proverbs 17:22)

Your mind is the receptacle and storehouse of God's counsel

> "I will bless the LORD who has given me counsel;
> My heart also instructs me in the night seasons.
> I have set the LORD always before me
>   [He is always in my mind];
> Because He is at my right hand I shall not be moved.
> Therefore my heart is glad . . . "   (Psalm 16:7–9)

Your mind is the place out of which you are instructed to communicate your undivided love to God

> "...love the LORD your God with all your heart, with all your soul, and with all your strength." (Deuteronomy 6:5)

> "As for you, my son Solomon, know the God of your father, and serve Him with a loyal heart and with a willing mind; for the LORD searches all hearts and understands all the intent of the thoughts. If you seek Him, He will be found by you; but if you forsake Him, He will cast you off forever." (1 Chronicles 28:9)

Your state of mind towards the Lord determines the depth of relationship you experience with Him

> "LORD God of Israel, there is no God in heaven above or on earth below like You, who keep Your covenant and mercy with Your servants who walk before You with all their hearts [with an undivided mind]." (1 Kings 8:23)

The mind of the Lord is set on you

> "What is man, that You should exalt him,
> That You should set Your heart on him,
> That You should visit him every morning?" (Job 7:17–18)

God is looking to see if you will love Him by giving Him your full focus and attention

> "For the eyes of the LORD run to and fro throughout the whole earth, to show Himself strong on behalf of those whose heart is loyal to Him." (2 Chronicles 16:9)

Your mind is the place that God touches when He wants to move you into action; and it is the place where you decide to respond to that call

> *"Then everyone came whose heart was stirred, and everyone whose spirit was willing, and they brought the LORD's offering for the work of the tabernacle of meeting ... They came, both men and women, as many as had a willing heart ... And all the women whose hearts stirred with wisdom ... "*　　　　(Exodus 35:21–22, 26)

You are responsible to set your mind to seek the Lord; a mind unprepared is open to demonic attack

> *"And he [Rehoboam] did evil, because he did not prepare his heart to seek the LORD."*　　　　(2 Chronicles 12:14)

> *"Nevertheless good things are found in you [Jehoshaphat], in that you have removed the wooden images from the land, and have prepared your heart to seek God."*　　　　(2 Chronicles 19:3)

Your mind without the presence of the Lord is inclined towards evil

> *"And the LORD smelled a soothing aroma. Then the LORD said in His heart [His mind], 'I will never again curse the ground for man's sake, although the imagination* [yeser: inclination, desire, motive, thought pattern, plans and purposes formed in the mind] *of man's heart [mind] is evil from his youth."*　　　　(Genesis 8:21)

> *"A deceived heart* [AMP: *"a deluded mind"*] *has turned him aside; And he cannot deliver his soul ... "*　　　　(Isaiah 44:20)

Your mind can turn your spirit away from God

> *"Why does your heart carry you away,*
> *And what do your eyes wink at,*

That you turn your spirit against God,
And let such words come out of your mouth?"   (Job 15:12–13)

Your mind is the place where internal anguish, discouragement, and fear can enter and operate in your life

"Then their hearts failed them and they were afraid."
(Genesis 42:28)

The fall of Satan took place in his mind

"Your heart was lifted up because of your beauty;
You corrupted your wisdom for the sake of your splendour."
(Ezekiel 28:17)

Hardness and division in your mind will cause you to fall into trouble

"Happy is the man who is always reverent,
But he who hardens his heart [refuses to follow
    the way of the LORD] *will fall into calamity."*
(Proverbs 28:14)

"Son of man, these men have set up their idols in their hearts, and put before them that which causes them to stumble into iniquity. Should I let Myself be inquired of at all by them? Therefore speak to them, and say to them, 'Thus says the LORD God: "Everyone of the house of Israel who sets up his idols in his heart, and puts before him what causes him to stumble into iniquity, and then comes to the prophet, I the LORD will answer him who comes, according to the multitude of his idols, that I may seize the house of Israel by their heart, because they are all estranged from Me by their idols." ' "
(Ezekiel 14:3–5)

Your mind can be captured

> *"So Absalom stole the hearts of the men of Israel."*
>
> (2 Samuel 15:6)

You are divided when you say words that do not line up with your inner thought life

> *" 'Judah has not turned to Me with her whole heart, but in pretence,'*
> *says the LORD."*   (Jeremiah 3:10)

> *"Inasmuch as these people draw near with their mouths*
> *And honour Me with their lips,*
> *But have removed their hearts far from Me."*   (Isaiah 29:13)

> *"They speak idly everyone with his neighbour;*
> *With flattering lips and a double heart they speak."* (Psalm 12:2)

> *"How can you say, 'I love you,' when your heart* [whole mind] *is*
> *not with me?"*   (Judges 16:15)

Your mind is the place where both pride and humility operate

> *"But Hezekiah did not repay according to the favour shown him, for*
> *his heart was lifted up; therefore wrath was looming over him and*
> *over Judah and Jerusalem. Then Hezekiah humbled himself for the*
> *pride of his heart, he and the inhabitants of Jerusalem, so that the*
> *wrath of the LORD did not come upon them in the days of*
> *Hezekiah."*   (2 Chronicles 32:25–26)

God sometimes withdraws from you in order to test your mindset towards Him

> *"God withdrew from him, in order to test him that He might know*
> *all that was in his heart."*   (2 Chronicles 32:31)

The Lord experiences anguish and grief in His mind

> "Then the Lord saw that the wickedness of man was great in the
> earth, and that every intent of the thoughts of his heart [his mind]
> was only evil continually. And the Lord was sorry that He had
> made man on the earth, and He was grieved [filled with pain] in
> His heart [mind]."   (Genesis 6:5–6)

*Your mind is the place where the Holy Spirit convicts you of sin
through your conscience*

> "And David's heart [mind] condemned him after he had numbered
> the people."   (2 Samuel 24:10)

*Your mind is the place where decisions take place for repentance
and restoration to God*

> "And when they return to You with all their heart [with an
> undivided mind] and with all their soul in the land of their enemies
> who led them away captive ... then hear in heaven Your dwelling
> place their prayer and their supplications, and maintain their cause,
> and forgive Your people who have sinned against You, and all their
> transgressions which they have transgressed against you ... "
>   (1 Kings 8:48–50)

> "But from there you will seek the Lord your God, and you will
> find Him if you seek Him with all your heart and with all your
> soul. When you are in distress, and all these things come upon
> you in the latter days, when you turn to the Lord your God and
> obey His voice (for the Lord your God is a merciful God), He
> will not forsake you nor destroy you, nor forget the covenant of
> your fathers which He swore to them."
>   (Deuteronomy 4:29–31)

"Hear me, O LORD, hear me, that this people may know that You are the LORD God, and that You have turned their hearts back to You again."   (1 Kings 18:37)

"Circumcise yourselves to the LORD,
And take away the foreskins of your hearts . . . "   (Jeremiah 4:4)

" 'Now, therefore,' says the LORD,
'Turn to Me with all your heart,
With fasting, with weeping, and with mourning.'
So rend your heart, and not your garments;
Return to the LORD your God,
For He is gracious and merciful,
Slow to anger, and of great kindness."   (Joel 2:12–13)

God's cleansing and healing comes in accordance with the state of your mind towards Him

" 'May the good LORD provide atonement for everyone who prepares his heart to seek God, the LORD God of his fathers, though he is not cleansed according to the purification of the sanctuary.' And the LORD listened to the prayer of Hezekiah and healed the people."
                                 (2 Chronicles 30:18–20)

God can change your mind

" 'Then the Spirit of the LORD will come upon you, and you will prophesy with them and be turned into another man . . . So it was, when he had turned his back to go from Samuel, that God gave him another heart [mind]."   (1 Samuel 10:6, 9)

"Now the LORD said to Moses, 'Go in to Pharaoh; for I have hardened his heart [mind] and the hearts [minds] of his servants, that I may show these signs of Mine."   (Exodus 10:1)

"For it was the LORD *himself, who hardened their hearts* [minds]
to wage war against Israel." (Joshua 11:20 NIV)

God can enlarge your mind in an instant
In a dream at night the Lord asked Solomon:

*" 'What shall I give you?' And Solomon said: . . . 'Give to Your
servant an understanding heart to judge Your people, that I may
discern between good and evil.' "* (1 Kings 3:5, 9)

*"And God gave Solomon wisdom and exceedingly great understand-
ing and largeness of heart like the sand on the seashore."*
(1 Kings 4:29)

Your mind can be written upon and changed by you and by God

"I will put My law within them [qarab: inside within], *and on the
hearts* [minds] *will I write it; and I will be their God, and they shall
be My people."* (Jeremiah 31:33 AMP)

"Write them on the tablet of your heart [mind]*."* (Proverbs 3:3)

You have the responsibility to change and renew your mind

"Circumcise yourselves to the LORD,
And take away the foreskins of your hearts." (Jeremiah 4:4)

*"Therefore circumcise the foreskin of your heart, and be stiff-necked
no longer."* (Deuteronomy 10:16)

*" 'Cast away from you all the transgressions which you have
committed, and get yourselves a new heart and a new spirit. For
why should you die, O house of Israel? For I have no pleasure in the
death of one who dies,' says the Lord* GOD. *'Therefore turn and
live!' "* (Ezekiel 18:31–32)

The Mission and Ministry of the Messiah

In the New Testament the word "heart" is translated from the Greek word *kardia* and is *always* used figuratively to describe the mind, the soul, the seat of desires, feelings, affections and passions. In particular *kardia* is used to describe your belief system which operates in your subconscious mind and is responsible for driving your decision-making process and thus your actions. We shall see in this chapter that the New Covenant teachings of Jesus and the Apostles show us that the mind is both the centre of the activity of the Spirit of God and the enemy, and that the words that we speak and the actions that we take are all determined by the beliefs that we hold. These beliefs reveal the substance of who we are in the inner man.

"And He was handed the book of the prophet Isaiah. And when He had opened the book, He found the place where it was written:

'The Spirit of the LORD *is upon Me,*
Because He has anointed Me
To preach the gospel to the poor;
He has sent Me to heal the brokenhearted,
To proclaim liberty [freedom] *to the captives,*
And recovery of sight to the blind,

> *To set at liberty those who are oppressed;*
> *To proclaim the acceptable year of the* LORD.' "

(Luke 4:17–19)

This quotation used by the Lord about Himself is from Isaiah 61:1–2. In the original Hebrew the word translated "to bind up" is *habas* meaning "to bind, to wrap around, to cover, to bind up a wound, to bandage". The Hebrew for broken hearted is a combination of two words: *sabar* meaning "to break in pieces, to utterly crush and smash" (metaphorically it denotes a shattered mind), and *leb* which is also used to signify the mind. Regardless of outward appearance, this is the true condition of every human being according to the Word of God.

The Lord Jesus came to bind up our shattered
and broken minds.

Every person born into this world is poor, broken, utterly shattered, taken captive and imprisoned through the fall of Adam and Eve. The fall took place in the mind and consequently the poverty, brokenness, captivity and imprisonment of mankind is first and foremost in the mind. There is only one way out of this prison – the renewal of the mind through the ministry of the Lord Jesus Christ.

The Greek word for freedom or liberty in Luke 4 is *aphesis* and it means "to release, to forgive, the remission and forgiveness of sins". This sort of freedom can also only be given through one Person, the Lord Jesus Christ. He alone can bring freedom from the mental prison that is created through the consequences of sin and the work of the enemy.

The most amazing words in this text are that Jesus came to *"release the oppressed."* The word "release" is translated from three Greek words, the two key words being *aphesis*, meaning "to release, to forgive", and *apostello*, meaning "to commission, to send forth as an ambassador on a certain and specific mission" such as to preach the Gospel. Jesus did two things for you: He came to save you, forgive you, bind up your broken and shattered mind, to release you from poverty, *and also* to commission you for a specific purpose and mission in His Kingdom; in other words, He came to restore the purpose for your life. When He saved you, He saved you to the uttermost and heaven's call on your life is now activated and alive again through Him.

If you are oppressed today then you need to discover the purpose for which you are called. It is the lack of hope and vision that opens the door for oppression. This is a lie of the enemy I have seen over and over telling the children of God that there is no future, and no purpose for their lives. God's purpose for your life is part of, and is wrapped up in, your salvation.

Jesus came to bring healing and deliverance to your mind and as a result salvation, and restoration to the whole of your life, both now and into eternity, and a major part of this healing is the release of His vision for your life. Right now the Lord is working in you through your belief system, through your thoughts, through your ideas, through revelation; and He wants to do more. Your walk with Him is first and foremost worked out within your inner man, within your mind.

The defiled mind

Jesus' teachings also show us that it is the *kardia*, the mind of a man, that is defiled and the source of evil in an individual's life.

> *"Are you also still without understanding? Do you not yet understand that whatever enters the mouth goes into the stomach and is eliminated? But those things which proceed out of the mouth come*

> *from the heart [the kardia] and they defile a man. For out of the heart proceed evil thoughts, murders, adulteries, fornications, thefts, false witness, blasphemies . . . "*   (Matthew 15:16–19)

Every unclean and evil thing, sin itself, is conceived and developed in the mind.

So what does the New Testament teach to be the cause of this "defiled heart" within us and how does Jesus release us from it? In 1 John 3:5 we read, *"And you know that He was manifested to take away our sins"*, and in verse 8, *"He who sins is of the devil, for the devil has sinned from the beginning. For this purpose the Son of God was manifested, that He might destroy the works of the devil."* The coming of Jesus, all that He did, all that He said, His life, His death and His resurrection were for the purpose of taking away our sin and undoing, loosing, and destroying the works of the devil who is behind all sin. If we put this scripture alongside Luke 4:18–19 (Isaiah 61:1–2) we can see the twofold ministry of the Lord, on the one hand the destruction of the devil's work and on the other the healing and restoration of mankind.

How does Jesus destroy the work of the enemy?

In order to destroy the work of the enemy Jesus would have to undo the work that Satan started in the Garden of Eden and He would do this by being obedient to, and fulfilling the prophetic writings.

> *"Do you think I cannot call on my Father, and he will at once put at my disposal more than twelve legions of angels? But how then would the Scriptures be fulfilled that say it must happen in this way?"*
> (Matthew 26:53–54 NIV)

Jesus humbled Himself and came as a human being; He did not operate as God on earth, but submitted Himself as a man, as the second Adam, to His heavenly Father and His Word. Everything Jesus did was in accordance with the will of the Father and in fulfilment of the Scriptures, but spiritual activity takes place first in the brain and so Jesus Himself would have to fight and win the battle for His own mind; where Adam and Eve had failed, He must succeed.

After His baptism the Spirit of God led Him into the Wilderness and it was here that Jesus came face to face with Satan. This is the first time we see Satan, on earth, involved in an open discussion with a human being since the Garden of Eden. It is clear that a new order had arrived; because Jesus was born of a virgin He was not of the blood line of Adam, He was not a fallen human being, He was without sin, which is why Satan spent forty days attempting to break into the mind of the Son of God.

Just as in the Garden of Eden, the plan was the same; the words that Satan spoke and the vision of the world that he revealed to Jesus were carefully crafted and designed in an attempt to place a second thought in His mind, and to get Jesus to break and operate outside the Word that God had given to mankind. But Jesus resisted the enemy, and the weapon He used is the same weapon that is available to you and me today, the Word of God. Jesus' mind was in complete submission and obedience to the Holy Spirit and the Word of God; He had no doubt or unbelief in Him. Jesus is our example; submit to the Spirit, believe in the Word and you will experience His victory in the battle for your mind.

It is in another garden, the Garden of Gethsemane, that we see most clearly the ferocious battle Jesus fought in His own mind. That night Jesus was in intense turmoil; He described His own soul as being sorrowful to the point of death. He longed for the support and company of His closest disciples, but they slept. Alone, He endured the mental onslaught of the enemy; the Lord alone knows what was going through His mind that night.

> *"And being in anguish, he prayed more earnestly, and his sweat was*
> *like drops of blood falling to the ground."*   (Luke 22:44 NIV)

The Greek word translated as "anguish" is *agonia* meaning "a contest, a conflict". It depicts the intense anxiety, tension and dread experienced before a battle. This night the salvation of mankind was dependent on Jesus having the strength of mind to overcome this moment and hold to the will of the Father for His life. Praise God that Jesus had that strength!

It was in the Garden of Gethsemane that the battle was won. When He arose from prayer His mind was settled. He was going to the cross. The Word of God tells us in Isaiah 53 that Jesus was

> *". . . wounded for our transgressions,*
> *He was bruised for our iniquities,*
> *The chastisement for our peace was upon Him,*
> *And by His stripes we are healed.*
> *All we like sheep have gone astray;*
> *We have turned, every one, to our own way;*
> *And the* LORD *has laid upon Him the iniquity of us all.*
> *He was oppressed and He was afflicted,*
> *Yet He opened not His mouth;*
> *He was led as a lamb to the slaughter,*
> *And as a sheep before its shearers is silent,*
> *So He opened not his mouth . . .*
> *Because He had done no violence,*
> *Nor was any deceit in His mouth."*   (Isaiah 53:5–7, 9)

The Lord Jesus went to the cross for all the sins that we have wilfully committed, and for all the sins we have committed unknowingly through ignorance and deception. On the cross He was paying the price for the defilement of our minds and the reason the Spirit of God can dwell in your mind today is because of the sacrifice of the sinless body and blood of the

Lord Jesus that was given for you. The shed blood of Jesus fulfilled every requirement under Levitical law for blood sacrifices. Every sin is paid for and washed away; the blood of the Lord Jesus has cleansed you to the uttermost in God's sight. This is why His holy Presence can now come and live within you. Sin is committed in the mind, defilement takes place in the mind and redemption takes place in the mind through *believing* in the name and person of the Lord Jesus.

The Glory of God has returned to the temple. You are His temple; He lives in you, in your *kardia*, which is your mind. The works of the devil in the Garden of Eden were destroyed on the cross, but you have freewill and therefore, to experience the victory of the cross of Jesus and His deliverance, and the manifestation of all the promises of God in your life, you must work with His Spirit. He wants to totally transform your life through the renewing of your entire thought processes and belief system, until the mind of Christ is fully manifested in you and Satan is crushed under your feet.

Inner peace

Jesus knows about the battles that we face within and He has made a way for us to have peace. In fact He has commanded us not to worry or be anxious anymore; He would not give us a command unless He was going to make it possible for us to keep it. In the Upper Room on the night before the crucifixion Jesus gave important teachings and instructions to His disciples. He was not a Man given to repeating Himself and yet twice in chapter 14 of John's Gospel Jesus gave this same command:

> *"Do not let your hearts be troubled. Trust in God; trust also in me."*
> (John 14:1 NIV)

"Peace I leave with you; my peace I give you. I do not give to you as the world gives. Do not let your hearts be troubled, and do not be afraid."   (John 14:27 NIV)

Why specifically is it so important to be at peace? What is happening when we worry and experience anxiety?

In Matthew 6:25–34 Jesus teaches,

"Therefore I say to you, do not worry about your life, what you will eat or what you will drink; nor about your body, what you will put on. Is not life more than food and the body more than clothing? Look at the birds of the air, for they neither sow nor reap nor gather into barns; yet your heavenly Father feeds them. Are you not of more value than they? Which of you by worrying can add one cubit to his stature?

So why do you worry about clothing? Consider the lilies of the field, how they grow: they neither toil nor spin; and yet I say to you that even Solomon in all his glory was not arrayed like one of these. Now if God clothes the grass of the field, which today is, and tomorrow is thrown into the oven, will He not much more clothe you, O you of little faith?

Therefore do not worry, saying, 'What shall we eat?' or 'What shall we drink?' or 'What shall we wear?' For after these things the Gentiles seek. For your heavenly Father knows that you need all these things. But seek first the kingdom of God and His right-eousness, and all these things shall be added to you. Therefore do not worry about tomorrow, for tomorrow will worry about its own things. Sufficient for the day is its own trouble."

In this passage Jesus gives us a very deep revelation as to how to live free from inner turmoil. This is very important teaching, because at the root of all worry is fear, and 2 Timothy 1:7 tells us *"For God has not given us a spirit of fear, but of power and of love and of a sound mind."* Fear about life comes from the enemy; he is behind all worry and anxiety. In

Matthew 6:30 Jesus makes the statement that His listeners were of little faith. Anxiety and worry will destroy your faith. Worrying about life shows that we are divided in our thinking, doubting the promises of God, double-minded and in unbelief. Jesus teaches that you overcome worry and fear and open the door for provision by putting your total focus on the Kingdom of God and His righteousness. This is so important to grasp because the Lord wants to perform His promises in your life but He cannot work when you are anxious and worrying; you must trust Him.

In Matthew 21:21–22 Jesus makes this even clearer,

> *"Assuredly, I say to you, if you have faith and do not doubt, [diakrino], you will not only do what was done to the fig tree, but also if you say to this mountain, 'Be removed and cast into the sea,' it will be done. And whatever things you ask in prayer, believing, you will receive."*

If you totally believe, and do not doubt, or have *diakrino* meaning "to doubt, to be divided", you will see His power at work. But what we are so often unaware of, is that if we are worrying and anxious then we are in unbelief. Unbelief leads to worry, worry to anxiety, and anxiety left unchecked will lead us into depression, which is the full manifestation of doubt in God's Word. Remember, the anointing that is upon Jesus is an anointing to bind up broken, divided minds; He wants you free from fear, free from worry, free from anxiety, free from depression, free from anything that holds you captive in your thinking.

Whatever it is you need from the Lord, wherever the breakthrough needs to take place in your life, your mind is the place where God will sow His Word. The enemy wants to steal God's Word from you, and he does this by attacking your thought life; Jesus makes this clear in the parable of the sower. To those by the wayside *"the devil comes and takes away the word out of their hearts [kardia], lest they should believe and be saved"* (Luke 8:12). This verse does not only apply to the initial decision involved in salvation, it relates to every current and future situation in your life in which you will need the Word of God to bring you the salvation of God.

How does Satan steal the word out of your heart? By giving you a second thought, a doubt, *diakrino*, which unchecked will create a divided mind. We can know the Lord, love the Lord and still be bound by certain circumstances through doubt and unbelief in areas of our minds. And this is the danger zone because when the Word of salvation comes, if you are divided in your thinking, then the Word will be of no profit to you.

> *"But let him ask in faith, with no doubting [diakrino], for he who doubts [diakrino] is like a wave of the sea driven and tossed by the wind. For let not that man suppose that he will receive **anything** from the Lord; he is a double-minded man unstable in all his ways."*
> (James 1:6–8, emphasis added)

Here is an example. A very special lady who I had the privilege of coaching was in a critical and desperate situation. She had attempted to take her own life on more than two occasions. She was not eating or washing or taking care of herself, and was living a reclusive life. Days would pass by without ever getting off the sofa or even drawing the curtains to let in the light of day. She loved the Lord deeply, and daily listened to the preaching of the Word on Christian television. She read her Bible, she prayed, but she could not get a breakthrough. She was going deeper and deeper into captivity, living in what she described as a self-imposed prison. Why? Because the enemy was lying to her; daily she had a voice in her mind telling her she was a failure, telling her there was no hope for her future, that her life was over. Now this lady believed in the Lord and she believed in His Word but this self-talk within had divided her mind and, unbeknown to her, was preventing her from receiving the Word of God that would create her breakthrough and deliverance. This form of attack is subtle, it is as if you are talking to yourself, but the true source and end result of negative self-talk is destructive, devastating and evil.

Within six weeks of putting into practice the principles of biblical coaching this lady's life went through a complete 180 degree turnaround. The negative self-talk was silenced, the negative beliefs broken, the demonic strongholds removed from her mind and the power of the Word of God was manifest in her life physically through the work of the Holy Spirit. She experienced complete deliverance from depression and suicidal thoughts and to this day she has never looked back, she is becoming stronger every day, she has hope for her future and is now ministering to others in difficulty.

We have seen through the ministry of Jesus that the only solution for mankind is to believe in Him and receive the presence of His Holy Spirit into the heart of the problem, within our minds. Doctors treat millions of people for depression but no tablet or prescription can set people free from this oppression. It is impossible, because the problem is not physical but spiritual. We are now going to look at the ministry of the Spirit as He works out the redemptive plan of the Father within us. Child of God, there is work to be done in your mind and the Holy Spirit is with you to perform the miracle of transformation. Your heavenly Father knew you before you were formed (see Psalm 139:13). He knows your purpose and He sent and gave His own Son so that you could be redeemed, released to fulfil the purpose that He has planned for you, and to be who He created you to be.

The Ministry of the Spirit

James' story...

James had almost reached the top of his profession, when he suffered a complete mental breakdown which resulted in him having to stop work, leave his job and step down from his position on the leadership team in the church. The guilt and self-doubt that followed the breakdown led him deeper and deeper into depression; this professional, bright, educated man ended up self-harming and thinking of taking his own life.

Every night in the early hours he would wake up and start to worry about losing control in his job; fear had totally gripped him and finally his system could not take the emotional pressure any longer and he experienced a mental breakdown. At the time when we first spoke he was at the point where he was self-harming and had suicidal thoughts running through his mind.

This precious man of God is born-again, filled with the Spirit, he loves the Lord, he reads the Word, he prays, so how on earth did he end up like this?

Seed time and harvest

James' problems all began with a single thought; seeds of doubt entered into his mind through negative words, which were empty of faith and contrary to the Word of God. This single thought was the beginning of the satanic assignment designed for the purpose of destroying James' life.

James did not realise who was at the source of a negative fearful thought like this or what it was created to do and so the thought was left unchecked. He started to worry, which meant he had now moved into unbelief and was therefore operating in his old nature which is under the control of the enemy. The negative thought became stronger and stronger until it became a negative belief, a "stronghold" in James' mind. This demonic belief became a reality to James' subconscious mind and so now began controlling his feelings, his emotions, his outlook, his perception on life and finally his spoken words; he started to speak death over himself.

The thought that James would lose control in his job produced worry; worry led James to experience anxiety, anxiety built on worry until it turned into depression; depression brought with it a whole set of even deadlier thoughts and beliefs of its own, and here is the deception: James did end up losing control, not in his job, but in his mind, and therefore in his life.

James is a prime example of how Satan gets a foothold in a believer's life, through the small beginnings of a tiny seed of thought that is negative or contrary to the Word of God. James' experience shows us how a person unconsciously falls more and more into bondage through their thought life until the demonic force is finally in the position where it is actually able to lead that person into self-harm and ultimately suicide, first spiritually and then naturally. This, child of God, is the full harvest of negative or destructive words and beliefs.

James is a Spirit-filled believer. How is the enemy able to lead believers in the Lord into destruction? He does it by causing them to operate in their old belief system or by creating a belief that is contrary to the Word, both of which are under his control. Biblical coaching enables you to completely break such strongholds in your mind. After only four weeks of coaching James was able to write the following testimony:

"A few weeks ago I was back in the midst of a desperate cycle of anxiety and depression. I wasn't sleeping, and I was crying a lot. Whilst I knew and would have said that I have a great deal to be thankful for in my wonderful family I was directionless and had lost all hope for my future. I had lost a career and a well-paid job in education, and just couldn't see how I could ever be in a position to make a worthwhile contribution again. I was aware that the Bible is a 'Gospel of peace' but unable to experience the manifestation of that peace in my life.

That was when a friend put my in touch with Lesley. The Lord has used her ministry to give me my hope for the future back. Two months ago I would have said, 'I can't see my future and I am very anxious about it.' Now, through much concentration on speaking out what the Bible says about my life, I find that generally my spirit has lifted. I am sleeping better and for the most part my tears have dried up. I am working to replace the negative voice that has tormented me with the positive affirmations in Scripture. I carry a little book around in my pocket, in which I have a number of scriptures and I use this to speak out the truth that God says about my life whenever the negative voice returns. I feel I am getting stronger every day and I have had several occasions when great excitement has welled up in me regarding the future.

What is interesting to me is that I have been able to identify one of the sources of the tidal wave of anxiety that used to hit me concerning my work and future. I had been listening to lies that set themselves up against the Word of God. I was double-minded.

I have made a great deal of progress and I am excited about what the Lord is doing. It's not over yet; I still have times of anxiety, but I am determined to keep on deleting the lies, and under God to renew my mind. I am very thankful to Him for what has happened so far, and looking forward for what He has for me!"

✤   ✤   ✤

Jesus taught us in John 10:10 that Satan comes to steal, kill and destroy life, but we have been largely ignorant of one of the major ways that he does this. Just as in the Garden of Eden, it begins initially with very subtle and deceptive words which can come in the form of a single thought that is contrary to the Word of God. These thoughts are carefully crafted to lead us into unbelief or sin and consequently render our faith ineffective. Today the lives of many believers are being destroyed because they do not realise and identify who is at the source of negative thinking and worry, and many people do not want to acknowledge that there is a demonic influence behind the mental battles, unbelief and sin in their lives. But the Word of God is black and white on this point, and this is why we must look to the Scriptures for the truth and the solution.

The mind of Adam and the mind of Messiah

The first question we must ask is how does the enemy get into our minds? The answer is he already has access to the natural, carnal, fallen mind we were born with through Adam, which is why the New Testament puts such huge emphasis on renewing the mind, putting on the "new man" and having a mind set after the Spirit.

Before we were born again our minds were totally blinded by Satan and we could not see the Kingdom of God, but the moment the word of faith came and we believed in Jesus, light entered our minds and literally pierced and penetrated the darkness of our carnal minds with the knowledge of God. Suddenly the veil was lifted and we could see what was previously invisible, the Kingdom of God.

> *"But even if our gospel is veiled, it is veiled to those who are perishing, whose **minds** the god of this age has **blinded**, who do not **believe**, lest the light of the gospel of the glory of Christ, who is the image of God, should shine on them ... For it is the God who commanded light to shine out of the darkness, who has shone in our **hearts**, to give the light of the **knowledge** of the glory of God in the face of Jesus Christ."*
>
> (2 Corinthians 4:3–4, 6, emphasis added)

There are two key points for us to draw from this text; firstly that as believers we now have the light of the knowledge of Jesus Christ shining in our minds, but this light is shining out of the darkness. The darkness here is referring to our unredeemed belief system, which the Bible describes as the carnal mind, the mind set on the flesh, the old man; this is the fallen mind we inherited as human beings descended from Adam.

This scripture reveals that apart from the knowledge of Jesus everything else within our minds is in fact darkness, which means that there is absolutely nothing good about the knowledge we receive outside and apart from the knowledge of Him. It is for this reason that the Holy Spirit is now residing within our minds, and His mission is to expand our knowledge of God more and more, until Jesus is fully formed in us. This process of transformation takes place through the renewing of our minds and it is absolutely critical because this is how we grow in the Lord and experience His victory over Satan in our lives.

The second point in this scripture is that Satan, who is described here as *"the god of this age"*, has power to blind the minds of unbelievers. In this particular text Paul is describing those who have not as yet come to faith in the Lord Jesus; however the word translated "unbeliever" (*apistos*), was used by the Lord Himself when he spoke to Thomas after His resurrection, and in this case *apistos* was used to address and correct a believer who had moved from belief into unbelief.

In the Greek *apistos* means "a thing not believed, to doubt, not to have faith or belief". In John 20:27 Jesus commanded Thomas, *"Stop doubting and believe"* (NIV). What Jesus is saying here is, "Change your state, stop having unbelief (*apistos*) and have belief (*pistos*) in Me." Child of God, whenever you are worrying, anxious and speaking negative destructive language, internally or externally, you have *apistos* and have moved from belief back into unbelief. And as we have seen, unbelief exposes us to work of the enemy. He is the author of *apistos* (doubt in God), because he speaks words that create thoughts that create beliefs that are contrary to the knowledge and the Word of God.

Jesus instructed Thomas to change his state (*ginomai*), to literally change his mind and have *pistos* which is specific faith in Him. If He commanded Thomas to change his mind then Thomas must have been the one who had the power to do it. Freewill gave Thomas, and gives you, that power to move from unbelief into belief, from the carnal mind to the mind set on the Spirit. It is a freewill choice.

So as believers we have the light of the knowledge of God in our minds but we also have darkness, which is our old nature rooted in our un-renewed belief system, which is built on knowledge that is contrary to God's Word. It is within this un-renewed belief system that the enemy works in a believer's life. The Spirit of God is building a new belief system through the renewing of your mind, that you might grow to live and make all your decisions according to Him by the Word and the revelation knowledge He brings which is always in perfect agreement with the Scriptures.

Two kinds of knowledge

Just as there are two minds, the mind set on the Spirit and the mind set on the flesh, so there are two types of knowledge and two types of wisdom. The first two chapters of 1 Corinthians teach us about the knowledge and wisdom of the world and the knowledge and wisdom of God. Worldly wisdom and knowledge bring nothing but darkness to our minds because it is not from the Lord, it is from below and it is earthly, un-spiritual and demonic. The wisdom of this world is under the control of Satan because it originates from him. It is a form of knowledge that is totally contrary to the knowledge that comes from God, and totally contrary to the Word of God.

> *"Such 'wisdom' does not come down from heaven but is earthly, unspiritual, of the devil. For where you have envy and selfish ambition, there you find disorder and every evil practice. But the wisdom that comes from heaven is first of all pure; then peace-loving, considerate, submissive, full of mercy and good fruit, impartial and sincere."* (James 3:15–17 NIV)

At one point your mind operated solely in the knowledge and wisdom of the world, but at the point of salvation you received the Spirit of God and with Him the beginnings of a totally new belief system that is utterly contrary to your natural mind. The Holy Spirit wants to work with you to cut out or put off the old man, which is the old mindset that operates in worldly knowledge and wisdom; He does this by building a completely new belief system in your brain which grows and grows as you receive more and more knowledge of God.

> *"... since you have put off the old man with his deeds, and have put*
> *on the new man who is **renewed in knowledge** according to the*
> *image of Him who created him."*
>
> (Colossians 3:9–10, emphasis added)

You put on the new man, the Lord Jesus Christ, through the
Spirit by renewing your mind with the knowledge of God that
He brings directly from the mind of the Lord (1 Corinthians
2:10–16) and from the Word of God. Without this renewal
process you cannot and will not grow or experience the power
and promises of God in your life; even worse, if you do not
renew your mind then you will continue to operate in the old
belief system to which the enemy has access, and this is how
Satan retains a position in your mind and therefore in your
life. You must pull down his strongholds by crucifying the old
belief system and the old nature it creates.

> *"But you have not so learned Christ, if indeed you have heard Him*
> *and have been taught by Him, as the truth is in Jesus: that you put*
> *off, concerning your former conduct, the old man* [the un-renewed
> mind set on the flesh] *which grows corrupt according to the*
> *deceitful lusts and be renewed in the spirit of your mind."*
>
> (Ephesians 4:20–23)

A believer's mind

We have the Spirit of God living in our minds, and through
Him we have received the mind of Christ. We have the light
of the knowledge of God shining in our minds. So why are so
many believers suffering from depression? Why do we
experience such internal conflict? Why do we not see more
answer to prayer and the power of God flowing through our
lives?

In the opening chapter of the first epistle to the Corinthians,
Paul tells the believers:

*"I thank my God always concerning you for the grace of God which was given to you by Christ Jesus, that you were enriched in every thing by Him in all **utterance** and all **knowledge**, even as the testimony of Christ was confirmed in you, so that you come short in no [spiritual] gift, eagerly waiting for the revelation of our Lord Jesus, who will also confirm you to the end, that you may be blameless in the day of our Lord Jesus Christ."*

(1 Corinthians 1:4–8, emphasis added)

Paul makes a connection here between receiving the knowledge of God, the ability to communicate that knowledge through speech, and operating in the gifts of the Spirit. However, he then goes on to plead with the Corinthian believers to stay in unity by having *"the same mind"*:

"Now I plead with you, brethren, by the name of our Lord Jesus Christ, that you all speak the same thing and that there be no divisions among you, but that you be perfectly joined together in the same mind and in the same judgment."   (1 Corinthians 1:10)

Having pointed out that spiritual gifts operate out of the mind, Paul now makes clear that the same mind that received knowledge and spiritual gifts from God also has the ability to become divided, carnal and of the old nature, the flesh, and this is exactly what had happened with the Corinthians. One moment they were operating in the Spirit, in the new nature created by the new belief system, and the next they were in the flesh, the old nature, created by the old belief system. Paul refers to them as babes in Christ, because maturity produces unity in the Church and is the corporate result of individuals who have renewed their minds.

"And I, brethren, could not speak to you as to spiritual people but as to carnal, as to babes in Christ. I fed you with milk and not with solid food: for until now you were not able to receive it, and even

*now you are still not able; for you are still carnal. For where there
are envy, strife, and divisions among you, are you not carnal and
behaving like mere men?"* (1 Corinthians 3:1–3)

In the book of Romans Paul speaks further of the two
mindsets, a mind set on the Spirit and a mind set on the flesh.
This is in fact a description of two different belief systems. As
believers, when we experience confusion, worry, and anxiety
it is because we are experiencing duplicity or a double mind
which is in fact the result of holding two viewpoints as truth at
the same time. We are actually operating in two opposing
belief systems at the same time, the mind set on the Spirit,
which is the new belief system under the power of God, and
the mind set on the flesh, the old belief system, which is under
the power of Satan. For example, you consciously set your
mind on the Spirit, reading your Bible, praying, worshipping
and believing God for a breakthrough in an area of your
life and then the next moment you are worrying about a
situation, doubting God, anxious about life, all of which is the
result of the old belief system which is under the power of
the enemy.

It is for this reason we see unanswered prayer and
experience a powerless Christian walk. It is impossible for
the power of the Spirit to flow through and break a demonic
situation in our lives when we are still operating in the belief
system that created the problem. Worry, anxiety and negative
words are all fruit of beliefs that are under the power of the
enemy.

The Holy Spirit longs to set you free from the old nature
because it destroys your life and restricts His power to
perform His Word. He does not want you to live in confusion
and the torment of doubt, which comes from operating in the
old nature; He wants to bring you peace in your mind, but His
peace only comes from the certainty that God's Word and
promises are sure, and that certainty is the fruit of a renewed

mind. He wants you to exercise His power and authority over Satan in every area of your life, but this is impossible if you are still operating in Satan's system, the old nature.

The mind set on the Spirit

> " *'Eye has not seen, nor ear heard,*
> *Nor have entered into the heart* [kardia] *of man*
> *The things which God has prepared for those who love Him.'*
>
> *But God has revealed them to us through His Spirit, for the Spirit searches all things, yes, the deep things of God."*
>
> (1 Corinthians 2:9–10)

These verses and the ones that follow teach us about the knowledge of God, our minds, our spirits, God's mind and God's Spirit. Just like God, our own spirit searches us, and *knows* us because our spirit is connected to and joined to our mind. If the Spirit of God is living and working in your mind then where is your spirit? Your spirit is also at the core of your mind, now joined to the Lord for those who believe. *"But he who is joined to the Lord is one spirit with Him"* (1 Corinthians 6:17).

We learn in the book of Hebrews 4:12 that the Word of God is sharper than any two-edged sword, dividing between joint and marrow, soul and spirit. This is a picture of the mind and the spirit. Just as the marrow sits inside the joint, so your spirit sits inside your soul. Your soul is your mind, your character, who you are, and this is another reason why renewing your mind is critical. Your redeemed nature is eternal. Just like the Father who created you, your spirit is at the centre of your mind.

In 1 Corinthians 2:12–13 we go on to read:

> *"Now we have received, not the spirit of the world, but the Spirit who is from God, that we might* **know** *the things that have been*

*freely given to us by God. These things we also **speak**, not in words*
which man's wisdom teaches, but which the Holy Spirit teaches,
***comparing** spiritual things with spiritual."*   (emphasis added)

The Holy Spirit brings you knowledge directly from the mind of the Father and this, child of God, is the revelation knowledge you are created to live, move and breath in; this is how the Lord Jesus operated, by receiving knowledge from the Holy Spirit who searches the mind of the Father. Any knowledge outside of this is in fact darkness and from the enemy.

A clear example of this is in Matthew 16:13–23. Jesus asks His disciples who they think He is and Peter answers, *"You are the Christ, the Son of the living God"* (v. 16). Jesus replies, *"Blessed are you, Simon Bar-Jonah, for flesh and blood has not revealed this to you, but My Father who is in heaven"* (v. 17). Peter has just received a revelation directly from the Father in heaven through the Spirit of God. But immediately afterwards Peter takes Jesus aside and starts to rebuke Him about speaking of His death; Jesus turns and says to Peter, *"Get behind Me Satan! You are an offense to Me, for you are not mindful of the things of God, but the things of men"* (v. 23).

In one moment Peter was speaking to Jesus out of revelation knowledge that came from the Father. In the next moment he was speaking from carnal knowledge, from his fallen nature and understanding, and Jesus immediately identified where this came from, and directly rebuked Satan. Peter had a divided mind, and whenever we have a divided mind as believers, we will step outside the will and Word of God.

Satan was working directly through Peter by putting thoughts in his mind that were based on a form of knowledge that was contrary to the Word of God. This is the knowledge and wisdom of the world, which he controls. Jesus identifies Satan as the source of such thoughts and words, and that it is Satan himself who has a mindset that is contrary to the Scriptures and the Spirit of God (compare with Romans 8:7 NIV: *"the sinful mind is hostile to God. It does not submit to God's law, nor can it do so."*). All thoughts and beliefs which oppose God's Word and purpose for your life come from the same source, the enemy.

Putting on the "new man"

In order to operate by the Spirit in revelation knowledge, and in accordance with the Word of God, action is now required on your part. Paul points this out in Ephesians 4:20–24:

> *"But you have not so **learned** Christ, if indeed you have heard Him and been taught by Him, as the truth is in Jesus: that you put off, concerning your former conduct, the old man which grows corrupt according to deceitful lusts and **be renewed in the spirit of your mind**, and that you put on the new man* [the result of renewing the mind] *which was created according to God, in true right- eousness and holiness."*   (emphasis added)

Note here that putting off the old man and putting on the new is an activity that you must perform. In Titus 3:5 we read, *"according to His mercy He saved us, through the washing of regeneration and renewing of the Holy Spirit."* So here we see that it is the Holy Spirit who actually performs the renewing but He does not do it alone. We see from scriptures such as Ephesians 4:22–24 and Romans 12:2 that you have to work with Him to enable this transformation process to take place. Child of God, without your work and involvement nothing is going to change.

Do you want to see the power of the cross fully at work in your life? Do you want to experience all the promises in the Word of God that Jesus has won for you? Do you want to see the enemy crushed under your feet, answered prayer and the power of God working in your life? Yes! Then now is the time to commit to work with the Holy Spirit. In the following chapters you are going to learn the practical biblical skills that will enable you to apply the teaching from the scriptures we have covered, in your own life. You are going to learn *how* to renew your mind and open the way for the Holy Spirit to pour Himself without measure into your life as He forms the very nature and person of the Lord Jesus in you. He will transform your life in a way far beyond what you could ever dream or imagine. I have seen it happen many times and if you stick with the process it will happen for you.

Ask the Lord to give you revelation and insight as you study the following scriptures.

The heart of man in the New Covenant

A pure mind enables you to see God

> *"Blessed are the pure in heart* [mind],
> *For they shall see God."*   (Matthew 5:8)

God can open your mind

> *"The Lord opened her* [Lydia's] *heart* [mind] *to respond to Paul's message."*   (Acts 16:14 NIV)

God searches your mind

> *"Now He who searches the hearts knows what the mind of the Spirit is."*   (Romans 8:27)

Your mind is the dwelling place of God

> *"At that day you will know that I am in My Father, and you in Me, and I in you . . . If anyone loves Me, he will keep My word; and My*

Father will love him, and We will come to him and make Our home
with him."   (John 14:20, 23)

"He anointed us, set his seal of ownership on us and put his Spirit in
our hearts [minds] as a desposit, guaranteeing what is to come."
                                    (2 Corinthians 1:21–22 NIV)

"And because you are sons, God has sent forth the Spirit of His Son
into your hearts, crying out, 'Abba, Father'!"   (Galatians 4:6)

"That He would grant you, according to the riches of His glory, to be
strengthened with might through His Spirit in the inner man, that
Christ may dwell in your hearts through faith."
                                        (Ephesians 3:16–17)

Your mind is the place where your faith resides and operates

"For assuredly, I say to you, whoever says to this mountain, 'Be
removed and be cast in to the sea,' and does not doubt in his heart,
but believes that those things he says will be done, he will have
whatever he says."   (Mark 11:23)

Satan can snatch God's word from your mind

"When anyone hears the word of the Kingdom, and does not
understand it, the wicked one comes and snatches away what was
sown in his heart. This is he who received seed by the wayside."
                                        (Matthew 13:19)

Satan seeks to blind your mind to the truth

"For the God of this world has blinded the unbelievers' minds (that
they should not discern the truth), preventing them from seeing the
illuminating light of the Gospel of the glory of Christ, the Messiah,
Who is the image and likeness of God." (2 Corinthians 4:4 AMP)

Satan can put his evil thoughts in your mind

> *"And supper being ended, the devil having already put it into the heart of Judas Iscariot, Simon's son, to betray Him . . . "*
>
> (John 13:2)

> *"But Peter said, 'Ananias, why has Satan filled your heart to lie to the Holy Spirit and keep back part of the price of the land for yourself?'"*
>
> (Acts 5:3)

Your belief system is the source of the words you speak and will create either blessing or curse in your life

> *"For out of the abundance of the heart the mouth speaks. A good man out of the treasure of his heart brings forth good things, and an evil man out of the evil treasure brings forth evil things. But I say to you that for every evil word men may speak, they will give account of it in the day of judgment. For by your words you will be justified, and by your words you will be condemned."*
>
> (Matthew 12:34–37)

Your mind is the place where God looks to see the truth about who you really are

> *"So My heavenly Father also will do to you if each of you, from his heart, does not forgive his brother his trespasses."*
>
> (Matthew 18:35)

Your thought life can defile you

> *"But those things which proceed out of the mouth come from the heart, and they defile a man. For out of the heart proceed evil thoughts, murders, adulteries, fornications, thefts, false witness, blasphemies. These are the things that defile a man . . . "*
>
> (Matthew 15:18–20)

A closed mind grieves the Lord and His Spirit

"And when He had looked around at them with anger, being grieved by the hardness of their hearts, He said to the man, 'Stretch out your hand.'" (Mark 3:5)

You can walk with the Lord and still have a closed mind

"Then He went up into the boat to them, and the wind ceased. And they were greatly amazed in themselves beyond measure, and marvelled. For they had not understood about the loaves, because their heart was hardened." (Mark 6:51–52)

"Why do you reason because you have no bread? Do you not yet perceive nor understand? Is your heart still hardened?" (Mark 8:17)

The Lord is One, He is totally united and He wants your undivided attention

"Jesus answered him, 'The first of all the commandments is: "Hear, O Israel, the LORD *our God, the* LORD *is one. And you shall love the* LORD *your God with all your heart, with all your soul, with all your mind, and with all your strength." This is the first commandment.'"* (Mark 12:29–30)

The Lord wants you to watch over your mind for your mind can be taken captive (excessive drinking affects our minds)

"But take heed to yourselves, lest your hearts become weighed down with carousing [over-indulgence in alcohol and other physical pleasures], *drunkenness, and the cares of this life and that Day come on you unexpectedly."* (Luke 21:34)

The Lord tests your mindset

> *"But as we have been approved by God to be entrusted with the gospel, even so we speak, not as pleasing men, but God who tests our hearts."*   (1 Thessalonians 2:4)

The Holy Spirit moves in your mind to bring you to salvation

> *"Now when they heard this, they were cut to the heart . . . "*
>   (Acts 2:37)

God purifies your mind through faith

> *"So God, who knows the heart, acknowledged them by giving them the Holy Spirit, just as He did to us, and made no distinction between us and them, purifying their hearts by faith."*
>   (Acts 15:8–9)

The Holy Spirit of God lives in your mind

> *"Who also has sealed us and given us the Spirit in our hearts as a guarantee."*   (2 Corinthians 1:22)

The Spirit of Jesus, the Son of God lives in your mind

> *"And because you are sons, God has sent forth the Spirit of His Son into your hearts, crying out, 'Abba, Father'!"*   (Galatians 4:6)

> *"That He would grant you, according to the riches of His glory, to be strengthened with might through His Spirit in the inner man, that Christ may dwell in your hearts through faith."*
>   (Ephesians 3:16–17)

Jesus wants your mind to be at peace and free from fear

"Let not your heart be troubled; you believe in God, believe also in Me."   (John 14:1)

"Peace I leave with you, My peace I give to you; not as the world gives do I give to you. Let not your heart be troubled, neither let it be afraid."   (John 14:27)

The Lord is the one who brings you peace of mind

"Now may our Lord Jesus Christ Himself, and our God and Father, who has loved us and given us everlasting consolation and good hope by grace, comfort your hearts and establish you in every good word and work."   (2 Thessalonians 2:16–17)

Preparing for Metamorphosis

6

> *"I beseech you therefore, brethren, by the mercies of God, that you present your bodies a living sacrifice, holy, acceptable to God, which is your reasonable service. And do not be conformed to this world, but be transformed by the renewing of your mind, that you may prove what is that good and acceptable and perfect will of God."*
>
> (Romans 12:1–2)

The Bible tells us that when you were born again you received the mind of the Lord Jesus Christ through the Spirit (1 Corinthians 2:16). But there has to be a fusion, a transferral of His mind into your mind. This is the process of maturing as a believer, and this process involves you undertaking the critical job of renewing your mind. The whole aim of this is so that you can find out exactly what God wants for your life and agree with Him that His plan for you is good and well able to succeed. In order for this to happen, God requires you to use your freewill and the ability He created you with to renew your mind into thinking His way, in line with His Word so that He can pour His power into your life.

So why is it so important for you to renew your mind?

Quite simply if your mind is not renewed you will continue to
think the same old unregenerate thoughts. These thoughts are
contrary to the Word and opposed to the Holy Spirit.

> *"For those who live according to the flesh set their minds on the*
> *things of the flesh, but those who live according to the Spirit, the*
> *things of the Spirit."*   (Romans 8:5)

Your old thought life will lead you along the same old paths,
and those same old paths will get you the same old results.
Why? Because the actions you take every day are all based on
the decisions that you make. Your decisions are determined
by what you think and what you think is a result of what you
believe and value to be true.

Every bad and wrong action that you have ever taken in
your life came out of a bad decision that was the result of
wrong thinking, and every good and right action that you
have ever taken came out of a right decision that was the
result of right thinking. In the Kingdom of God right thinking
springs directly and only from a mind renewed by the Word
of God under the anointing and leading of the Spirit of God,
and these two are in perfect agreement – all of the time.

An un-renewed mind will think contrary to the Spirit and
the Word of God; it will think in favour of the flesh or
carnally. God urges you not to set your mind on the things
of the flesh but to set your mind on the things of the Spirit;
this is another way of saying "renew your mind" according
to the Word. Setting or renewing your mind on the things of
the Spirit will bring you life and peace and a life full of the
presence and power of the Lord.

The internal conflict we experience is the warring of the
enemy, through our flesh or our un-renewed mind, against
the Spirit and the Word of God. The Word of God promises,

"You will keep him in perfect peace, whose mind is stayed on You" (Isaiah 26:3). The only way to win this war and experience peace is to set our whole focus on the Lord and His Word, resisting any other voice, until the internal conflict stops. Internal conflict arises for two reasons: on the one hand your flesh, your un-renewed mind, desires to operate contrary to the Word, and behind this is the enemy of your soul who works to lead you into sin, unbelief and therefore bondage to him; whereas on the other hand the Holy Spirit is wanting to lead you into freedom, which He also does in your thought life by revealing sin and unbelief to you. He does this to call you to turn so that He can lead you into truth, forgiveness, healing and life according to the Word of God; all internal conflict is an indication that your mind needs to be renewed.

As a believer in the Lord Jesus you are in the midst of a battle, a battle for your mind, a fight for the Word of God in you. The Lord Jesus said that the Kingdom of God is within you and God has placed the power to change your world within you, but it takes a renewed mind to put to death the flesh and to access and release His power. Every breakthrough you will experience begins within you as a change of thought, a change of belief. And you are going to learn how to harness your mind and create breakthrough with the power that God has placed in you, in your inner man.

The key to the abundant life that Jesus has bought for you lies is in learning how to have an uninterrupted flow of the Holy Spirit in your life; beliefs, words and actions that are contrary to the Word of God interrupt this flow. The aim of renewing the mind is to remove these blockages so that Jesus can be fully formed in you.

So, where do you begin?

In preparing to move forward it is essential to recognize how your beliefs and thoughts have shaped your past and brought

you to where you are in life today. For me, I have seen that
every negative outcome in my life came as a result of taking
actions that were contrary to God's Word. And yes, you've
got it; those actions came as a result of wrong beliefs and
thoughts that came through deception and rebellion working
in my un-renewed mind.

The good news is that once you have awareness you have
begun the process of positioning yourself for breakthrough,
and once you start actively working on renewing your mind
you are then in line with the Word of God and engaged
with the Spirit of God who wants to release His power in
your life.

So now what about you? What is your story so far? What
decisions have you made, what have you believed about
yourself, others, life, and the Lord Himself to arrive at the
point where you are today? I want you to take some time for
yourself and work through the following questions. As you do
so, do not allow condemnation to come near you. All of the
exercises you are going to do as you work through this book
are leading you to one place – a fabulous and fulfilled
relationship with the Lord and a successful life in His
Kingdom. You are a child of God, you are deeply, deeply
loved. Believe it, it's true. Your heavenly Father is holding
your future in His hands and He has a master plan for you that
is awesome, beyond anything you could dream or imagine.

The purpose of these exercises is to help you to realise and
identify that what you were meditating on, what you had in
your mind, your thoughts, your beliefs, all shaped the
decisions that you made and drove the actions that you took.
Your beliefs have shaped your life, sometimes away from
the Father's plan. He can and will redeem everything that
went wrong. However, you do not want to make the same
mistakes twice ... do you? Working through these questions
diligently will reveal hidden beliefs and wrong thinking, which
are strongholds in your mind.

The devil wants strongholds to remain in your mind because this is how he keeps you in bondage; it is how he has access to you. The Lord wants these strongholds removed so that you can be renewed and secured into a future that is full of life, joy, peace and power in the Holy Spirit. He wants to lead you to a place where you operate only by the revelation knowledge that He gives you. Jesus only did what He saw the Father do; He lived every day by revelation knowledge. When we operate in our own understanding, and in our own knowledge, we will have a powerless life. The Father wants us to have a powerful life.

Heaven is full of overcomers, and you are an overcomer whether you feel like it or not because of the One who lives in you! It doesn't matter how bad your life may be right now, Jesus is alive and He is with you; His resurrection power is available to you today. If you are in a place right now where you barely have any strength left, just hold on, live another day because the same power that raised Jesus from the dead is available to you. The Holy Spirit is wonderful. He will carry you, He will lead you. Ask Him to talk to you now and to show you the truth. He has the solution, the answer and the way out of whatever you may be facing.

Action: Renewing your mind

Step 1: Awareness
This exercise is aimed at uncovering what you have believed and what you believe today about yourself, others, life and the Lord. The repetitive process will help you to identify the underlying beliefs that are driving your actions today, and enable you to discover how your life so far has been shaped and created by what you have believed to be true.

The key question to ask in any area of difficulty in your life is "What do I believe?" And does this belief line up with the Word of God? If not, where do you think it came from?

Awareness is the starting point for breakthrough; it is coming to the knowledge of the truth that will turn you around. The Holy Spirit wants to begin by showing you where you have been in deception so that He can lead you into the only true truth, the revelation of Jesus who is the Word of God.

Commit this exercise to the Lord, ask Him to bring truth to your mind, ask yourself the following questions and write down the answers in the blank spaces or even better buy a journal if possible to use as you work through the book.

What challenges am I facing today?

. . . .
. . . .
. . . .

What specific areas of my life are under pressure right now?

. . . .
. . . .
. . . .

What do I believe about myself in this situation? Do these beliefs line up with the Word of God?

. . . .
. . . .
. . . .

What do I believe about my circumstances? Do these beliefs line up with the Word of God?

. . . .
. . . .
. . . .

What do I believe about other people (if others are involved)? Do these beliefs line up with the Word of God?

. . . .
. . . .
. . . .

What do I believe about the Lord in this situation in my life? Do these beliefs line up with the Word of God?

. . . .
. . . .
. . . .

What decisions have I made based on these beliefs? Did these decisions line up with the Word of God?

. . . .
. . . .
. . . .

What result, what fruit (good or bad) have these decisions produced in my life right now?

. . . .
. . . .
. . . .

What actions have I taken based on my beliefs?

. . . .
. . . .
. . . .

What has happened as a result of taking these actions?

. . . .
. . . .

Based on my actions, does this area of my life line up with the Word of God?

. . . .

. . . .

✢ ✢ ✢

Having answered these questions, what can you see now? What are you learning? Write it down.

So what needs to change?

. . . .

. . . .

. . . .

How have your beliefs brought you to the place where you are in life today?

. . . .

. . . .

. . . .

What do you think will happen to you if you change your beliefs to line up with the Word of God?

. . . .

. . . .

What do you think must happen in order for your circumstances to change?

. . . .

. . . .

Take some time to pray over these answers, wait on the Lord and give Him time to minister to you.

Action: Root and fruit charts

Step 1: Reality today

Using the answers from the first exercise to help you, you are now going to take a more detailed look at specific areas of your life. This is meant to be repetitive. By continuing to ask the same questions in a slightly different way you will uncover more specific beliefs.

Complete the charts on pages 85–86 beginning with *Chart 1: Today*. For each area of your life ask yourself again, what am I thinking? What do I believe about myself, this area of my life, the Lord, people? What actions am I taking as a result of those beliefs? Do my beliefs and actions line up with the Word of God? What is the result of my actions? What fruit is in my life today? Write down the answers in your journal or in the blank spaces, and add any extra areas of your life to the chart as necessary. In the scale box, write a figure between 0 and 10 (0 being that you have nothing in this area and 10 your life is blessed and totally in line with the Word of God).

Step 2: Finding hope for your future

In the next chapter you are going to move on to look at your future, and now you are going to take a small step towards identifying goals for each area of your life. To do this you need hope. I have been in a situation where if it had not been for the Word of God and the promise of His redemption from every mistake in my life I would have given up hope. This is a dark place to be. But you and I must remember that we pass *through* the valley of the shadow of death, we don't stay there. The work you are doing now is taking you through; you are coming out, child of God. I don't know where you are at this moment, but no matter how desperate you feel, no matter how broken the situation is, no matter what you have or haven't done you are coming out, there is hope for your future, and there is new life ahead of you.

Lift up your head, focus on the Lord. I have prayed for you now as you read these words that the precious Holy Spirit will come to you, fill you with His presence and release vision.

Now look to the future and write down on *Chart 2: Future* on page 86 what is in your "heart", what comes from deep within your subconscious. We are not talking about fleshly selfish desires here; we are talking about life according to the Word of God, restored relationships, debt clearance, powerful anointed ministries, healed and healthy bodies, wholeness, sound minds, prosperous professional lives. So, if anything were possible what would your goals be for each area of your life? According to the Word of God what should be written in the score and sentence box? What beliefs do you think you will need for the Word of God to be fulfilled in each area of your life? Just write a brief sentence for now. *"God . . . calls those things which do not exist as though they did"* (Romans 4:17). The visible, natural impossibility of your current situation cannot hold you if you will trust the Lord, open up and let the *"desires of your heart"* come to the surface. Write them down now.

> *"Delight yourself also in the LORD.*
> *And He shall give you the desires of your heart."*   (Psalm 37:4)

From this moment in time, ignore every other voice, every doubt, every condemnation, and be a visionary.

Root and fruit chart 1: Today

Your life today	Scale 0–10	Describe your life, your beliefs and actions – do they line up with the Word?
Relationship with the Lord		
Mentally – what do you believe about yourself?		
Emotionally		
Family		
Husband or wife (if not married fill in your current relationship)		
Ministry		
Friends & social life/ Fun & relaxation		
Business/Career/ Work		
Finances/Income		
Living environment/ Home		
Physical – health, fitness and appearance		

Root and fruit chart 2: Future

My future hope	Scale 0–10	According to the Word, what will my life be like? What must I believe?
Relationship with the Lord		
Mentally – what must you believe about yourself?		
Emotionally		
Family		
Husband or wife (if not married fill in your current relationship)		
Ministry		
Friends & social life / Fun & relaxation		
Business / Career / Work		
Finances / Income		
Living environment / Home		
Physical – health, fitness and appearance		

Biblical Coaching in Practice

The first step is to daily seek the Lord for His plan for your life. Secondly you must then work on goals for each area of your life, in light of God's plan for you, by putting each one through a simple goal setting process. This process is essential, as it immediately brings to the surface all the unidentified, hidden, negative and limiting thoughts you hold about yourself, other people, your situation, your life, and most importantly, about the Lord and His power to save you. Getting rid of these strongholds in your thinking is central to renewing your mind and moving your life forward.

All negative thoughts and beliefs are fear based and have a power attached to them that is designed to drain away your faith. At the root of any fearful negative thought is a spirit of fear and behind the spirit of fear is the devil himself; he is fear.

God does not want you to have fear. The Bible tells us that *"God has not given us a spirit of fear, but of power and of love and of a sound mind"* (2 Timothy 1:7). When you have fear in your mind you will be divided and you cannot operate in faith when you are double-minded (see James 1:5–8). Always remember, the strategy of the devil is to get you away from serving God with a whole heart. He wants to divide your mind and get you to doubt the Word so that he can drain away your faith and prevent the power of God from flowing through your life.

Fear must be removed from your mind. You do this by uncovering faithless beliefs and replacing them with beliefs that are in line with the Word of God for your life. As you set goals with the Lord, He will uncover and reveal any fear in you so that you can be set free. He wants to do this for you, because fear left unchecked will eventually cause mental and spiritual paralysis.

> *"Now the Lord is the Spirit; and where the Spirit of the Lord is there is* **liberty.**'   (2 Corinthians 3:17, emphasis added)

> *"God is love . . . There is no fear in love; but perfect love casts out fear.'*   (1 John 4:8, 18)

The Lord Jesus is with you now to deliver you from past fear and failure. As you do your part and faithfully work through the process you are about to learn, the Lord will do His work and set you free from whatever has held you and kept you bound; it is time to put the past behind you.

What exactly is a goal?

A goal is a specific aim or objective to be reached. Goals are the milestones that enable you to fulfil the vision God has for your life. Goals have a set place in time when they are to be fulfilled. Goals are a living unseen substance that eventually manifest in fulfilment in the physical visible realm of this world.

Two biblical principles for goal setting

Firstly the Word of God tells us in Proverbs that without vision the people perish (see Proverbs 29:18 KJV). Why do people perish without vision? Because human beings were created to live by revelation, by vision from the Father; people need a purpose in life. As a believer in the Lord, vision is a revelation from the Spirit of the purpose of God for your life, and this knowledge will keep you focused and carry you through the external pressure and trials you will face in this world as a believer. Without vision you will be influenced by the natural world around you, and you will live and be moved by what you see.

The Word tells us that the just shall live by faith. Children of God are not supposed to live by what they see physically, but by what they see by faith. The enemy works in two ways through your physical sight, either to tempt you with someone or something, to lead you into sin, or to get you to focus on the physical and natural impossibilities of your situation rather than promises of the Word of God for your life, in order to lead you into unbelief. The vision and purpose of God for your life is always much bigger than any natural circumstance you could possibly face and is always of infinite value that far outweighs anything that this world has to offer, and this is why you need this revelation from the Lord.

The psalmist writes:

> *"Turn away my eyes from looking at worthless things,*
> *And revive me in Your way."* (Psalm 119:37)

The way to guard yourself from visual temptations is to develop the inner vision and goals for your life. In his book, *The Fourth Dimension*, Pastor Yonggi Cho tells of how for a certain period of his life he spent more time with his eyes shut than open so as to protect the vision God had put in his heart.

The second principle regards action. Once you have a vision, a revelation, you must act. Jesus said that the man who

hears His words and does them is like a man who built his
house on a rock, and when the storms came the house stood.
His life was secure. Equally, the man who hears what Jesus
says and does not act, his house, his life, will be swept away
when the storms come (see Luke 6:46–49).

The principle for us to grasp here is that it is not hearing
what Jesus says that will save your life, but hearing and acting
on what He says. This principle applies to goal setting; it is not
only identifying and writing down a goal that will bring
change in to your life, but identifying and acting on that goal.
Once you have a vision you must act upon it to activate it and
keep it alive. This world will crowd in and choke the vision if
you do not act.

Perhaps the most powerful revelation regarding action is to
be found in the book of James:

> *"You believe that there is one God. You do well. Even the demons*
> *believe – and tremble! But do you want to know, O foolish man, that*
> *faith without works is dead? Was not Abraham our father justified*
> *by works when he offered Isaac his son on the altar? Do you see that*
> *faith was working together with his works, and by works faith was*
> *made perfect?"*   (James 2:19–22)

Having faith, having a vision, is not enough. You must take
action because it is acting on your faith that will activate your
faith, and perfect and bring into physical reality the vision
from God. This is how your internal vision works itself out
and manifests in the physical world. Works does not simply
mean carrying out good deeds for others; binding Isaac to the
altar in order to sacrifice him to God was not a good deed for
Isaac. No, it was an act of faith on behalf of Abraham who
trusted that God would raise his son from the dead because of
the promise Abraham had received from the Lord to make
him the father of many nations.

What does God say in His Word regarding goals?

"But one thing I do: Forgetting what is behind and straining towards what is ahead, I press on towards the goal to win the prize for which God has called me heavenwards in Christ Jesus."

(Philippians 3:13–14 NIV)

Goals are mini visions that compound to fulfil the ultimate vision for your life, and they are biblical. All the great men and women of faith had goals, and these goals were attached to vision, specific vision. The Word tells us that the Lord Jesus endured the cross for the joy that was set before Him (Hebrews 12:2). Jesus knew exactly why He was here and what He was called to do. He knew the vision for His life, He had the revelation from His Father, and this vision carried Him through the torture of the cross.

In all His suffering He focused on the fulfilment of His vision, the salvation of mankind. This is the joy that carried Him through. Jesus was fully convinced in His mind that the Father's plan for His life would be fulfilled and that all who would believe in Him would be restored to the Father. The intense joy of this vision gave Him the strength of mind to endure the cross and fulfil His purpose on earth.

Jesus overcame and took ground from the devil throughout His entire time of ministry; His movements here on earth were not random; there was a very clear plan of action for His life. There were specific goals in His life that had to be reached in order for prophecy to be fulfilled, and ultimately the Word was leading Him to the cross and the final fulfilment of the purpose of His first coming on earth. It is the same for you and me. Your life has a purpose; Psalm 139:16 tells us that all our days were written in a book before the foundation of the world. God has a written plan according to His vision for you and attached to this vision are specific goals that will lead you to the fulfilment of your purpose on earth.

Right now Jesus is alive in you, He is still the Man of vision, He is still absolutely focused and He holds the detailed written plan of the goals and ultimate purpose for your life. It is not a hit and miss affair, there is a mandate from heaven for you, and whether you realise it or not, you are carrying it within you right now. You already have the DNA for success, because of the One who is in you. The Lord does not want you wandering aimlessly through life. He wants you to discover your calling and He wants you to write it down.

Creating an action plan

"Write the vision
And make it plain on tablets . . .
For the vision is yet for an appointed time."   (Habakkuk 2:2–3)

A written plan for your life will keep you on course when the storms hit. God-breathed goals converted into a written action plan will keep you focused when demonic attacks come against your life, which they will as the Word of God is fought for in you.

Inspired by the Spirit, men of God wrote down the plan of God for mankind. The Bible contains the revelation of the visions and goals of our heavenly Father, His written plan. He has not stopped writing! He wants you to form an action plan and write it down; this will get you moving and open a way for God to work His power in your life.

The devil also has goals; he is a strategist. He does not attack your life aimlessly; he also has a plan, a written plan. Paul warns us about the wiles of the devil (Ephesians 6:11). These wiles are strategies, carefully worked out plans. Child of God, setting goals engages you with the Spirit, and taking action releases the power of God to deliver you from the enemy.

Your goals are anchors and waypoints that fix you and keep you on the ordained path through the battles of life until you reach the final fulfilment of your purpose on earth. To go through life without goals would be like trying to sail a boat across the Atlantic Ocean without a map or a compass on a cloudy night. And to go through life with an idea of your goals, but never forming a written action plan, would be like getting your co-ordinates but never actually plotting your course on the chart. It would only be a matter of time before you were blown off course, lost, in extreme danger and ultimately shipwrecked.

The Word of God must be first and foremost in our lives, and fellowshipping with the Spirit in the Word is life. But there must then be an outworking of the revelation God gives you. If God has spoken to you, what are *you* going to do about it? Faith without works is dead. Remember you have the authority on earth. Jesus has given it to you, and goal setting is a way of working out the Word, working out the revelation, working out the vision in the authority that Jesus has given to you.

Discovering the Lord's vision for your life

God has placed within you a desire that He wants to fulfil through you; and therefore this deep desire is totally achievable no matter what situation you may be in at this moment in time.

Your struggle may simply be because you do not know your purpose in life, or you do know it but you are not yet running in *the* race that God has set for you. God created you for a very specific purpose, and it is essential that you find out exactly what this purpose is. When you discover why you are here and step out into the calling He has placed on your life, you will experience His blessing in every dimension of your life, in every area of health (physical, mental and emotional), in relationships, work, family, and yes, in finances. The Lord does not want you to remain broken, sick, homeless or in debt. He created you with gifts and abilities and when you find your purpose they will come alive in you. The anointing will flow and life will begin to work for you; you will begin to prosper.

For some of us the struggle comes because we have already gone off course. We failed, we fell, and the enemy gained a foothold in our lives. You may feel that your life is over. It is not over; it is never over with the Lord. He calls things that are not as though they were (Romans 4:17).

When you fall the real challenge is over who you are going to listen to from that point on. Will you listen to the devil, who will tell you that you are finished, and create physical circumstances that also talk to you and also tell you that you are finished? Or will you listen to the Spirit and the Word? Jesus has redeemed you from every lawless deed (Titus 2:14). He became sin that you might become the righteousness of God. If you turn and ask for forgiveness then you are free. Look at the life of King David and the events that occurred around his relationship with Bathsheba. Many today would say that he was finished, but God saw his heart and restored him. You are not finished, you are redeemed, beloved, and you are going to become a living testimony to this truth.

How does God reveal His vision for your life?

There are many ways that God can reveal His purpose to you. He can speak audibly to you as He did with Samuel; He can appear to you personally or in a vision as He did with Paul; He can send an angel as He did with Daniel; He can send a prophet as He did to David; He can even use animals as in the case of Balaam! However, He can also put vision directly into your heart which expresses itself through your desires. The book of Nehemiah does not record that God spoke to him before he went before the king to request that he be allowed to rebuild Jerusalem, but he had a vision in his heart and in Nehemiah 2:12 we read, *"I told no one what my God had put in my heart to do at Jerusalem."* It is recorded that Nehemiah prayed fervently throughout his ministry but there is no recorded reply from God. God was speaking directly into his heart all the time; and as you know, in biblical language your heart is your mind.

So now is your moment, now is the time to begin to find the purpose for your life. Before you move on to setting specific goals for your future, it is time to stop, be still and come before the Lord. This is the moment when, if you are not on the right path for your life, you can make a 180 degree turn and start heading in the right direction. Talk to Him now:

> "Father, I ask You to reveal to me Your plan for my life. Speak to me and show me Your purpose for my life. Where do I fit into Your plan? Father, I believe this is a new day for me, a new beginning; that You have brought me to this point in my life. Show me the desires You have placed within me. Father, show me how to start, what is the first step I need to take. Holy Spirit, I love You. I need You. I commit this time to You. I ask You to lead me now, Lord, into truth, the truth of how You see me, and Your wonderful plan for me and for Your redemption in every area of my life."

Take time, wait on the Lord, stay before Him in His presence, pray in the Spirit, be still and ask yourself the following questions. These questions are created to uncover desires that the Lord has already placed within you; remember you were made for a specific purpose and when you were born again that purpose was reactivated through and in the Lord Jesus. Each time you ask a question, pause, wait and write down the answer that comes into your mind. Do not stop to analyse what you hear, let the Lord speak to you. You have the Spirit

of God within you, He is with you, He made you and He will
speak to you through your thoughts. Shut out the world and
your current circumstances, ask and keep asking these questions and then write down what you hear, see or feel within.

If there were no obstacles, what would I be doing? What
else, and what else?

. . . .
. . . .
. . . .

What is my deepest desire?

. . . .
. . . .
. . . .

What is it that lies within me as an unfulfilled desire?

. . . .
. . . .
. . . .

What do I want to see happen in the world?

. . . .
. . . .
. . . .

What do I want to see happen in my life?

. . . .
. . . .

What gifts do I have?

. . . .
. . . .

How could I use these gifts to fulfil my deepest desire
and to bring about what I want to see happen in the
world and in my own life?

. . . .

. . . .

. . . .

Now use these answers to form a sentence or short paragraph
that summarises what you have discovered. His calling always
blesses others; He is going to bless you to be a blessing. The
vision for your life is your ministry in the Lord and the goals
you are about to set will lead you into the fulfilment of this
ministry.

This exercise will flush out all sorts of negative beliefs,
feelings and emotions. These are simply signals that are telling
you that there needs to be a change, a shift in your life. For
now I want you to write them down on a separate piece of
paper and put them to one side. You will learn how to deal
with the negative inner voice in the next chapter. For now
focus on the desire God has given you, *"What do you want?"*
The Lord Jesus asked blind Bartimaeus, *"What do you want me
to do for you?"* He asked him *"What do you want?"* Don't be
afraid of this question when you have submitted your desires
to the Lord.

Keep focusing on the vision. Inside you there is a hope, a
God-given desire, for your life which is far better and bigger
than what you are currently experiencing. It is simply the
gap between your internal visible world and your external
physical world that causes tension and emotional pain. The
goal setting process you are now going to learn will provide
you with an action plan for closing that gap by creating a
bridge from the spiritual, creative realm into the natural
physical world. This is what goal setting does, and this is why
it is so very important.

GRASP – the goal setting process

I am now going to introduce you to GRASP ©. This is a simple and yet powerful five-step goal setting process that is easy to remember, and if closely followed, will ensure that you goal set in a way that covers all the biblical truths we have covered so far in this book.

> Every element of this process is
> essential for breakthrough.

GRASP©

G = Goal
R = Reality
A = Actions
S = Set – set your mind
P = Proclamation

In the English dictionary, the true meaning of "grasp" is defined as: (1) a firm hold, (2) control or power, (3) the ability or opportunity to seize or attain something (success was within his grasp), (4) understanding or the ability to understand.

As you move forward with the Holy Spirit to work on your goal, it is good to be conscious of the fact that as you set a goal you are by faith:

1. Laying a firm hold on your future in accordance with the Word of God.
2. Using the authority, power and freewill that the Lord has given you to shape your life according to His plan.
3. Positioning yourself to grasp the opportunities that the Lord is going to release to you.

4. Renewing your mind with the Word of God, and so receiving the knowledge and understanding (beliefs and mindset) that you require, to reach your goal, and produce life and fruit in the Kingdom of God.

Across the top of a new page write down the sentence describing the vision you captured in the last exercise. You are now going to let this vision sit over all the goals that need to be set for each individual area of your life.

GRASP Step 1: G = Goal

Now once again dedicate this time to the Lord and ask the Holy Spirit to guide you. Trust Him and let go of any limiting thoughts.

Start with your Priority Goal first and complete the following five-step process. Look back at the notes from the "Root and Fruit charts" showing your life as it is today, and using the first draft of your goals to help you, decide which area of your life you want to work on first. What is it, if there could be a change today, that would bring the biggest impact to your whole life? This is a creative activity; by the Spirit see beyond your current circumstances, imagine that there are no obstacles in your way and in *accordance with the Word of God* ask yourself the following questions:

1. What specifically do I want for this area of my life?
2. How do I want my life to be?
3. What is the very best outcome I can imagine?

When you have the answers to these questions, I want you to define clearly into a sentence or short paragraph exactly what you hope for in this area of your life – this is your goal. As a believer you can attach to the goal you have just written this promise: *"God will do more than I can ever believe, dream, imagine or dare to ask for!"* (see Ephesians 3:20).

GRASP Step 2: R = Reality

R = Reality – create awareness. What is the current situation? What do you believe about the situation and what do you believe about yourself? What actions, if any, are you currently taking?

In a short sentence or paragraph, write down the current situation in this area of your life.

GRASP Step 3: A = Action

Now ask yourself, "What can I do to close the gap between where I am right now and where I want to be?" List all the options that come to mind and then ask yourself, "What else can I do?"

Keep asking and answering this question over and over until you have at least five or six options. List all the options that you have, but don't want to take. List crazy options! Crazy often precedes creative. Please think outside your comfort zone at this point, and keep asking, "What else can I do to achieve this goal, what else, what else, what else?" It is this process of open questioning that creates the opportunity for the Holy Spirit to speak to you and show you above and beyond what you currently think is possible. Give the Holy Spirit time to speak to you. He will give you new ideas. Keep asking yourself, "What else can I do?"

GRASP Step 4: S = Set

In the English dictionary the word "set" is defined as: to put something in a particular position, to place it deliberately and carefully, to decide on and fix, to perform, to put something that is broken or dislocated back into its right position; to become solid, resolutely intending to do something, determined and immovable.

From your list of options now ask yourself, "What *will* I do and when will I do it?" Choose the actions that you are going to take. Now set the date and time when you will act. Take any actions you can now – immediately, do something today, now. Write the date and, where possible, time when you will act. Commit to this before the Lord and before a friend if possible. Give yourself absolutely no way out.

Your actions open the way for the Holy Spirit to create breakthroughs. This is the moment you put faith into action with your works, and this is how you build momentum. You *must* take action. If you do nothing, then nothing will change. If you take action the Lord will create change. He does not work without you. Remember, Jesus said, *"Go and make disciples ... And surely I am with you always"* (Matthew 28:19– 20 NIV). Signs and wonders follow the preaching of the Word and signs and wonders will follow your *acts* of faith. Taking action on your goal is an act of faith.

You must initiate the action:

> *"Ask, and it will be given to you; seek, and you will find; knock, and it will be opened to you. For everyone who asks receives, and he who seeks finds, and to him who knocks it will be opened."*
>
> (Matthew 7:7–8)

GRASP Step 5: P = Proclamation

The final stage of goal setting is to capture the negative thoughts that are arising in your mind, together with any fear, by writing down exactly what you are saying to yourself at this point. In biblical coaching goal setting is designed to flush out limiting, negative beliefs; this is a very important and essential part of the process. Take five minutes to write down everything that is running through your mind at this moment concerning you and the fulfilment of this goal.

These thoughts are in fact the keys to the proclamations and affirmations that are required to renew your mind. The negative thoughts that come to mind at this point, together with feelings of fear or anxiety, are the evidence that a change needs to take place in your belief system. In the next chapter you are going to learn the skills that will equip you to make this change and renew your mind.

Once a goal is clearly identified, written down and acted upon it will actually affect your physical vision. You will start to see people, opportunities, resources etc. that the Lord has placed around you for the fulfilment of your goal. Your eyes will be opened to see the provision God has already put in the earth for you.

Your Subconscious Mind and the Power at Work in Your Words

In the last chapter you captured the negative thoughts that arose as a result of setting your goals. These negative thoughts are expressed in the form of a negative and fearful internal dialogue, which in turn affects your feelings and emotions, and is the fruit or evidence that at some point you have believed something that is contrary to the Word of God. This negative self-talk then works itself out into your spoken words, and from here it creates destructive results in your life because according to the Word, *"Death and life are in the power of the tongue"* (Proverbs 18:21). Life and death are in your words, internal and external.

Negative self-talk comes out of your belief system which is what the Bible refers to as your heart. It is for this reason that your internal dialogue is so important, because it reveals what is really going on within you at the centre of you.

Negative self-talk creates negative beliefs that drive negative actions that produce negative outcomes in your life. This negative cycle will keep you behaving in negative repetitive patterns according to the negative belief you hold about yourself. Because words give meaning to your experiences in life and create your beliefs, they are ultimately the seed and the source behind the actions you take every day of your life. It is for this reason that Jesus said, *"For by your words you will be justified, and by your words you will be condemned"* (Matthew 12:37).

For a believer, negative beliefs are deadly because they close down your ability to see the promises and blessings of God in your life and lead you into more unbelief. They also shut out the power of God because the Lord cannot work where there is unbelief. A negative belief will cause your mind to become closed to the Word of God, it will colour your perception and prevent you from learning key truths from difficult experiences that would otherwise have enabled you to succeed in the future. And so, when an opportunity or a new idea comes from the Lord, unbelief will rise up and prevent you from moving forward. Ultimately it can cause you to experience mental paralysis when it comes to trying anything new and will keep you locked into your past performance, and therefore experience.

A dear man that I coached had reached a point in his life where his emotions were in tatters. On the day we first spoke he could hardly string a sentence together without being reduced to tears. When I asked him what he was saying to himself about his life he told me, "My life is over, I am fifty-four and it's too late for me to make anything of my life now. Everything in my life is a mess, every time I try something I make myself ill. I can't do this, why bother?" These words had formed powerful negative beliefs that were ruling his emotions and controlling his life. When I asked him what he wanted he said, "I want to get my life back."

This man is an extremely talented musician and having changed his internal dialogue he has now been set free from his negative beliefs, his actions have changed, he is able to get on and enjoy his life again, and he is currently working on recording his first worship album.

Can you see the power that this internal voice has over a person's life? I have seen in every person I have coached that behind the physical problems there are a series of negative beliefs such as these. Following are some examples of situations you may be facing.

You may have struggled academically at school and not achieved very good qualifications, if any. As a result you may believe that you are not very bright, or you may even be telling yourself you are stupid or something worse. You may believe you have failed to live a fruitful life that you have made too many mistakes, and you may be telling yourself that, "It's too late now to find my purpose, my life is over."

You may be in a marriage that is struggling. Perhaps you are no longer in love with your husband or wife. You may believe that nothing is going to change, and be telling yourself, "I have to get out, there must be something better than this. I can't live like this any more."

You may be stuck in a job that you don't want to do. You may believe that this is it for the rest of your life. You may be telling yourself, "There is nothing better, I can't get out, I am stuck, I can't change jobs, and I don't have any options."

You may have fallen and committed sin as a believer. You may believe that the call on your life is over. You may have feelings of guilt and condemnation. You may be telling yourself, "I have blown it, the Lord will not trust me again, no one will trust me again, it's hopeless."

All these examples are taken from real situations in the lives of people I have worked with. And by the time they came to me the negative self-talk they experienced had led them to the point of breakdown, suicide, divorce, and for others to a place of self-loathing, desperation, depression and hopelessness.

Whatever it is that has happened to you, if you have faith in the Lord Jesus, then your life is not over. It is never over in Him, nor indeed is His calling on your life.

"For the gifts and the calling of God are irrevocable."
(Romans 11:29)

However, in order to experience the Lord and the power of His Spirit, you must be set free from negative beliefs about His Word, His power, His love for you and His desire to work miracles in your life. Any negative belief you hold about yourself and your abilities is actually rooted in unbelief in the Word, and this is what most of us are unaware of; this is how we unintentionally become double-minded. For example, if you personally believe your life is over, but you also believe that Jesus came to give you life and give it to the full, then your unbelief cancels out your belief, and this is why so much of our prayer life is ineffective, because our personal negative beliefs divide us.

The personal negative beliefs we hold about ourselves come from our interpretations of bad experiences in the past or of something negative that was spoken to us. Perhaps a parent, a teacher, someone you thought was a friend, or someone you trusted or loved spoke negative and destructive words to you either as a child or an adult. If not rejected, these words can go deep into your subconscious and stay hidden within you for life. The source of all negative words and beliefs is the enemy.

The Bible says that everything is "Yes and Amen" in Jesus. This means that He is positive, constructive, creative, and a life-giver. The opposite is true of the devil. He is negative, he steals, he kills and he destroys (John 10:10). Our words are either life-giving or life-taking, depending on the source, and our job is to harness our tongues and stop negative destructive words coming out of our mouths and running through our minds if we want to fully experience the presence of God in our lives.

James 3:2 tells us:

> *"We all stumble in many ways. If anyone is never at fault in what he says, he is a perfect man, able to keep his whole body in check."*
>
> (NIV)

He goes on to say in verses 9–12:

> "With the tongue we praise our Lord and Father, and with it we curse men, who have been made in God's likeness. Out of the same mouth come praise and cursing. My brothers, this should not be. Can both fresh water and salt water flow from the same spring? My brothers, can a fig-tree bear olives, or a grapevine bear figs? Neither can a salt spring produce fresh water." (NIV)

Harnessing the tongue goes hand in hand with renewing the mind; one cannot work without the other, because we renew our mind with the Word of God and with our own words. We must understand that words are containers that carry power. When you open your mouth to speak you are releasing either the power of God to create life and bring blessing or the power of the enemy to bring destruction.

All words operate within and out of the mind through what we hear, what we think, what we see and give meaning to, through revelation from the Spirit. In order to understand just how words shape our lives we must take a brief look at the workings of the conscious and subconscious mind.

The conscious and subconscious mind

You only have one mind, but there are two distinct parts to your mind, the conscious and the subconscious. And, as we have already discussed, just as there are two parts to your mind, there are two parts to your life, your inner invisible world, your beliefs, your thoughts, your self-talk, and their outward manifestation which is your outer visible world, your spoken words and actions. The life you are experiencing is created and controlled through this order.

These two parts or sides of your brain perform different functions. Your conscious mind deals with what you are currently aware of at any moment in time. Your subconscious stores all your knowledge, memories and beliefs, and it is also responsible for running all the automatic functions of your body.

You reason and make all your decisions with your conscious mind. However, this reasoning and decision making is determined by your beliefs, values and memories, which are all stored in your subconscious. Therefore, it is your subconscious that drives your conscious thought life. And subsequently, it is your subconscious that is shaping your understanding of your visible world and experiences moment by moment. It is out of the beliefs held in your subconscious that you act on "automatic" pilot, such as taking action or speaking without a second thought. The negative patterns and destructive cycles that are currently operating in your life reside and flow out of your subconscious.

Your conscious mind is responsible for relaying truth, or perceived truth, and facts to your subconscious to store. And, everything that you have ever learned and experienced, that is all your knowledge, is held in your subconscious.

Information is transferred to your subconscious through a network of neural pathways. Neural pathways are like highways along which information travels; and the more you think about a particular thing, the stronger the neural pathway becomes, until learning is complete and a belief is established in your subconscious.

Here is a simple example of the natural learning process: when you first attempted to tie a shoe-lace, you had to concentrate very hard with the full focus of your conscious mind. At that point you had no references for tying a shoe-lace in your subconscious. At this stage you were fully aware that you were not yet able to tie the shoe-lace – this is called *conscious incompetence.*

When you reached the stage of successfully tying your shoe-lace for the first time, again with the full concentration of your conscious mind, you had learned how to tie the shoe-lace, but you still had to concentrate. You had reached the stage called *conscious competence*.

Finally, after much practise, you are now fully proficient at tying your shoe-lace. You can tie it with your eyes closed, you don't have to consciously think about the sequence of actions any more, and in fact you can do several other things whilst tying your shoe-lace. You have now reached the third level of learning which is called *unconscious competence*. Your sub-conscious has received all the information it needs to enable you to operate on automatic pilot. Your conscious mind can now sign off responsibility and any future performance of this task will be automatic and handled by your subconscious. Most of us have experienced this when driving!

Whatever information, or experience, your conscious mind receives as truth, whatever you habitually think about, will cause the development of neural pathways which transfer information to your subconscious to store as absolute fact to be acted upon. Practically, this helps and enables you in everyday life to unconsciously perform tasks, allowing your conscious mind to be free to learn and focus on new challenges and the world around you.

However, there is a downside to this learning process. Human beings live in a fallen world and with a natural mind that is in darkness, without the knowledge of God. The carnal mind does not operate naturally in principles such as forgive-ness, love, self-less living. Herein lies the problem; as believers we have received the mind of Christ (1 Corinthians 2:16), and yet we still have the old beliefs within us and this is what renewing the mind deals with, the death of old beliefs and the creation of new beliefs that line up with the Word of God.

When you become born again, depending on your age or the intensity of your experiences, you may well have half a lifetime or more of beliefs stored within your subconscious that are negative and absolutely contrary to the Word of God. This is why the Bible commands us to be transformed by the renewing of our minds. We have to deal with the old belief system, with the subconscious. If we don't, there will be no transformation and without transformation we cannot grow up into a mature man or woman in Christ.

Negative beliefs, stored deep in your subconscious, produce negative thoughts, destructive self-talk and low self-esteem in that particular area of your life. This destructive pattern will cause you to doubt yourself and God, which will lead to unbelief, unbelief will lead to fear, and fear will lead you into destructive situations and experiences in your life.

Your subconscious does not reason or argue, it accepts whatever your conscious mind tells it. Your subconscious cannot tell the difference between something real and something vividly imagined. This is why anxiety and worry are such enemies to your soul. Jesus said, *"Therefore I tell you, stop being perpetually uneasy (anxious and worried) about your life"* (Matthew 6:25 AMP). As you consistently think and worry about a problem, you form a neural pathway along which these thoughts are then transferred, as fact, to the subconscious. Your subconscious will believe the thing you are worrying about is absolutely real, and as we will see, this will cause you to believe, think and act in a way that is contrary to the Word, and this potentially can enable the enemy to cause whatever you are worrying about to actually manifest in some form in your life. This is why you hear people saying, "I knew this would happen to me", after an event that they have been worrying about for so long. Remember, your thoughts form the basis for your spoken words, internal and external, and your words either release the power of God to create life or the power of the enemy to bring destruction.

"Death and life are in the power of the tongue."   (Proverbs 18:21)

"The thief does not come except to steal, and to kill, and to destroy."
(John 10:10.

Quite simply, your subconscious was created to keep you believing, thinking and acting, according to what it has received as truth from your conscious mind. Before the fall, Adam's mind was in complete harmony with God; he had a pure, holy, undefiled thought life; no inner conflict. Imagine that. And that is what the Holy Spirit is seeking to do in you as you work with Him to renew your mind.

We have seen how the natural learning process works and how it can work against us. The good news is that by using the same learning processes of the conscious mind to access the subconscious, it is possible to break negative belief patterns, and establish new positive beliefs. This is achieved through building new neural pathways in exactly the same way as they are formed in the natural learning process. Renewing your mind is actually a physical transformation that takes place within your brain.

I have seen the Holy Spirit accelerate this renewal process in the minds of believers many times. In the space of six weeks I have seen people, on the verge of suicide, totally renewed, delivered from the enemy (who works through negative beliefs), and restored to life in Jesus. This is the miracle of renewal, because without the Holy Spirit there is actually no true freedom from fear in the mind of a human being, because only in the Lord Jesus do we have victory over the enemy.

Satan binds people with the negative, lifeless words he puts into their minds, which in professional circles is termed called "self-talk", but you have to ask who is behind such "self-talk". Is it really you speaking or is it dressed up to appear that way? What I have seen is that this personal dialogue left unchecked has taken a lot of the people I have worked with to the brink of physical death. I know therefore that destructive self-talk is from the enemy because he is the one who comes to steal, kill and destroy your life. Many people today are ignorant of his tactics because they are unaware of the power that indwells their words and therefore shapes their lives. Your tongue has power, not because of what it is, but because of what it can do – speak words that can release the life of God or death and destruction from the enemy.

The Lord is the author of life and He wants to set you free; decide today that you will only speak life over yourself from this point on. Make this moment your turning point.

So how do you break a negative cycle?

You do this by impressing the Lord's plan for your life onto your subconscious through His Word, through proclamations and affirmations, through your internal and external spoken words, and through seeing your future from the Lord's perspective.

Breaking a negative cycle is simple, and you do it with the Word of God and with your own words by speaking the positive, constructive opposite of your or anyone else's destructive negative words.

Breaking the cycle

Step 1: Identification

The first step is to identify any negative beliefs you currently have. It is time to re-visit your goals, and to look again at the limiting thoughts you identified in Steps 2 and 5 of the GRASP© model.

Goal setting will flush out negative beliefs, but you can also identify them by how you are feeling. If you are feeling low, anxious, bad tempered, fearful, ask yourself, "What are the thoughts behind these feelings?", or "What am I saying to myself?" Feelings and emotions are attached to your belief system, and therefore if you are experiencing negative emotions the first step is to ask, "What is it that I believe, that is causing these emotions to surface?" Write down the answer.

Step 2: Words of life

So what is a "proclamation"? In biblical coaching a proclamation is a Bible verse that counteracts the negative words you have been speaking to yourself. For example, if you have been deceived into saying to yourself, "I have blown it, my life is over, I will never break free/get out of this situation", your proclamation might be something like, "Thank You, Lord, that You are my redeemer, and that You have redeemed me from every lawless deed" (Titus 2:14). 'Thank You, Lord Jesus, that You came to give me life and life in abundance" (John 10:10). This is applying the truth of the Word of God to break the lie of unbelief from the enemy.

An affirmation is a positive, present tense, personal statement about you that lines up with the truth of your proclamation, according to what the Word says about you. For example in this case you might say, "I have a second chance, this is a new day. I am starting afresh, I have broken free and I am on my way out of this situation."

An affirmation must be personal, positive and in the present tense. For example, you don't say to yourself, "The Lord is going to heal me." Instead you declare, "The Lord *is* healing me", because He is. That may take time but healing is in the Atonement, and *'By His stripes we are healed'* (Isaiah 53:5). This is the truth according to the Word. Jesus has already provided for your healing, and to receive the truth of this word into your mind, and therefore into your body, you declare the truth to your subconscious because it is a fact. In fact, right now healing is available to you if you fulfil the biblical conditions and are in faith to receive it. So you speak words of faith to your subconscious that you shall fully recover (Mark 16:18).

So, now it is time to go to the Word, to pray and ask the Lord to bring into your mind relevant scriptures that counteract your negative beliefs. Write them down; these verses will become your proclamations.

Now look at yourself through the cross, forgiven, washed,

whole, empowered by the Holy Spirit. In the light of who you are in Jesus, look at what you have been saying about yourself and now ask, "What must I believe about the Lord, His Word, and myself to move forward, to see this goal fulfilled?" Another way of phrasing this would be, "When this goal is fulfilled, what will I believe, and how will I feel?" Write these answers down; these will become your affirmations.

Child of God, this is awesome. What you are doing now is going to shape your life and your destiny. This is so powerful, I pray that you will grasp in the Spirit what is about to happen. If you have been oppressed, depressed, crushed by sin, the Lord is about to undo the works of the devil right now. This is the beginning of your deliverance.

Step 3: Pattern interrupt

The next step is to interrupt your negative self-talk cycle with your proclamations and affirmations. You do this by silencing

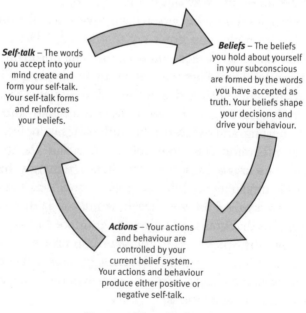

Self-talk – The words you accept into your mind create and form your self-talk. Your self-talk forms and reinforces your beliefs.

Beliefs – The beliefs you hold about yourself in your subconscious are formed by the words you have accepted as truth. Your beliefs shape your decisions and drive your behaviour.

Actions – Your actions and behaviour are controlled by your current belief system. Your actions and behaviour produce either positive or negative self-talk.

Diagram of the self-talk cycle

and deleting the old negative voice and replacing it with positive affirmations the moment negative self-talk begins, and especially immediately after a bad experience, behaviour, conversation and always when experiencing negative emotions and feelings.

If you have a negative cycle you interrupt the pattern by speaking your proclamations and affirmations (**P & As**) the moment the self-talk begins. If you act and behave wrongly, turn, ask forgiveness from the Lord and immediately speak out your P & As.

> This is a spiritual activity as well as a practical one
> because you are speaking life into a death cycle
> in order to break it.

Step 4: Practise and persistence
When and how often do you practise your proclamations and affirmations?
Write down all your goals, proclamations and affirmations in a small notebook and carry it with you at all times. As soon as you become conscious in the morning, I want you to think about the Lord's vision for your life and your goals, and then immediately start to speak your proclamations and affirmations, internally and preferably audibly. Pray, and ask the Lord to enable you to see your future through His eyes. Consider your goals fulfilled.

As you go through the day, the moment you start to feel a downturn, speak out and proclaim the Word of God together with your affirmations. Open your notebook and remind yourself of who you really are and where you are really going. Your proclamations and affirmations are a weapon; when you speak them you are declaring life over death. Pray, search the Scriptures and find other passages that support your goals. For example, if you goal is to come out of debt, find scriptures such as Jeremiah 29:11:

> *" 'For I know the plans I have for you,' declares the LORD, 'plans to prosper you and not to harm you, plans to give you hope and a future.' "*   (NIV)

If your goal is to be healed, Isaiah 53:5:

> *"By His stripes [**I am**] healed."*

If you are oppressed or depressed, Isaiah 61:1–2; Luke 4:18. If you have suffered self-hatred, and hate what you have done, find scriptures for forgiveness, redemption, restoration … whatever it is find it in the Word. The enemy will attack and when he comes, no matter how he manifests himself, deal with him immediately, ruthlessly, firstly with the Word and then speak out your affirmations. You are in the process of renewing your mind.

At lunch take five minutes to go through the process again, reviewing your goals, reminding yourself of the scriptures and speaking your affirmations. Close your eyes and see your future, bright, full of hope, your goals fulfilled. You are building the neural pathways, and making them stronger every time you do this. It is like going to the gym. Every time you work out you become stronger. The more you do it the greater and the quicker the results. Think of affirmations as feeding your soul – if you physically miss your meals, you become weak; it is exactly the same with your mind. In order to have a strong mind you must care for it and feed it high quality food.

> Remember, each time you proclaim the Word of God and speak out your affirmations the neural pathways in your brain develop more, and you become stronger.

As you go through the afternoon and evening keep your proclamations and affirmations in your consciousness. If the negative voice comes – destroy it! Immediately! Don't give it a second to speak to you. The devil comes to steal, kill and destroy. His words are death – don't allow him to speak. He will try to use your old belief system and initially it will intensify. Kill it off, use the Word and use your affirmations. You can do it; the Holy Spirit will give you the strength. Remember what happened when you were born again? He took up residence in your mind, He is there with you, He is in your mind and He will empower you to evict every destructive voice that arises.

When the battle becomes intense, start to thank God for every possible, conceivable thing in your life, and put on *"a garment of praise instead of a spirit of despair"* (Isaiah 61:3 NIV). The enemy hates you praising God, and he will flee from you. If you are in deep darkness, start to thank Jesus for the smallest things. Thank Him that for the air that you are breathing. Thank Him that He is with you in the darkness, then start to look for the light. Lift up your head, thank Him that you are passing through the valley, you are not staying there. Children of God don't stay in the valley of the Shadow of Death, they pass through it (Psalm 23). Thank Him that He has a table prepared for you, He has gone ahead of you and got things ready for the moment you come out of this oppression, because you are coming out. Thank Him that the enemy is defeated under your feet. Remember you are not alone; many others are going through what you are experiencing right now and when you come out you are going to be able to help them just as I am helping you now.

End the day just as you began. Remind yourself of who you really are, of where you are going, of the hope for your future. Proclaim the Word of God over your life, speak out your affirmations and fall asleep seeing your future according to the

Lord's vision for your life, think of the joy you will experience when your goals are fulfilled.

It is really important, whenever possible, to speak the scriptures and your affirmations out loud. It is such a powerful act to make an audible announcement to your mind and the physical and heavenly realm. Proclaiming the Word releases power, the power of God, and when the old negative self-talk starts up it is much easier to silence it immediately by speaking your affirmation out loud. You can try this for yourself. If you start to count to ten in your head and then speak your name out loud, the voice in your mind will stop. When you experience the old negative voice in your mind, speak out the Word and your affirmations and it will stop.

The fact that your proclamations and affirmations are not visible in the physical world right now does not matter, because it is your invisible, inner world that must transform first. This is living by faith and not by sight in practice. When the new belief is fully established in your subconscious, your mind will have been renewed according to the Word of God, and you will now be naturally speaking life to yourself; thoughts, emotions, decisions and actions that also line up with the Word will naturally follow. This mindset subjected to the Holy Spirit will result in you being one with the Word and the Spirit, which means that what you believe, what you say and what you do will be in perfect harmony with the will of the Father and it is at this point that the natural realm must and will yield to you as the Word of God manifests in your life in the physical visible realm. Hallelujah!

The change: What happens to you as you practise speaking positively?

On a purely physical level, speaking positively to yourself regularly throughout the day will build new neural pathways in your brain and, once strong enough, a new belief about yourself will be formed. As this happens the old neural pathway will die away and with that the old negative belief. This change can take place in anyone; you do not have to know the Lord to experience this level of change. But, this form of renewal does not lead to salvation, healing or deliverance from the enemy.

As a believer in the Lord Jesus, practising biblical positive and constructive self-talk is a spiritual activity that the Holy Spirit is deeply involved in. This is the action He needs you to take in order to do His miraculous work of renewing your mind. If you are faithful and persistent in the goal of uprooting the enemy from your thought life, the Holy Spirit will perform mighty works and the manifestation of His power in your life will become evident. I have seen this in the life of every person I have coached, every person. Anointed, biblical affirmations are the language of the Holy Spirit, because this is the language of faith, and He loves it, He is drawn to it and He creates the manifestation of the Lord Jesus in you through it.

Renewing your mind will lead you deeper and deeper in your walk with the Lord. The presence and activity of His Spirit will increase in your life, and as you shut down negative beliefs you will root out unbelief and so start to see more answers to prayer. Your spiritual sight will return as more light and revelation knowledge enters your mind, and you will see the purposes of the Lord becoming clearer and clearer to you.

Resisting the counterattack

Look again at the self-talk cycle diagram (see page 114). Just as you break a negative cycle with positive words, so the enemy will attempt to break a positive cycle with negative words. This is how he got a foothold in the first place, and he will attempt it again. This is where persistence comes in and we are going to look at this in more detail in the next chapter.

When you begin the process of renewing your mind, the negative self-talk usually intensifies initially. But very quickly the negative voice will weaken, as you get stronger through practising your proclamations and affirmations. Then a second form of attack comes which is usually a voice of doubt saying, "This is not working, it's pointless, nothing is changing, nothing is happening," and in the first person, "I don't feel any different, I am wasting my time," and so on. These words are designed to create a wave of negative emotions and feelings.

Ignore negative emotions and feelings.
This is not about feelings, it is about the living Word of God.
Stand firm and intensify your proclamations
and affirmations.

This second wave of attack means that everything is happening and everything is changing, the Word is working and you are being transformed. The fact that you are attacked with a voice of doubt actually means that the power of the enemy in your mind is in the process of being destroyed – think of a dam breaking. As soon as the first trickles of water break through, it is only a matter of time before the dam bursts. You are speaking life which is the living water of God's Word. It will break every stronghold if you just keep proclaiming and believe.

Remember, resisting this inner negative voice is resisting the enemy, and the promise of the Word is that as you resist the devil he will flee from you (James 4:7). A point will come when he will simply run away. Your job is to trust the Lord, stand on the Word of God and put into practice what you have learnt in this book. The Holy Spirit will do the rest!

Staying Focused

So, you have set your goals, identified negative beliefs and destructive patterns, written your proclamations and affirmations, and started the process of renewal. The question now is how do you stay on track every day? What do you do if the going gets really tough, when you can see no physical evidence of any progress? What do you do when the voice of doubt is hounding you and you feel like giving up? To answer these questions we must once again firstly look to the Word.

The Bible shows us that as human beings we are motivated by two opposite forces: pain and pleasure, and in Deuteronomy 28 we see these two opposite forces at work. This scripture warns us of the cost, the pain and the curses of disobedience, and reveals to us the joy, the pleasure, and the blessings of obeying God's Word. The Bible tells us that in His presence there are blessings for evermore. This is a motivator to pursue Him, because when we find Him we experience true joy, and true pleasure. To reject Him leads to separation, a cursed life, and ultimately death, and an eternity of pain.

The entire Bible works on these two principles: the joy, the blessings, the pleasure of knowing God, and the destruction and pain of rejecting Him. These two forces, pain and pleasure, drive our actions and motivate us on a daily basis, and when we become conscious of them, they become powerful forces that will enable us to stay on track with God, and with the purpose and goals He has for our lives.

When you come under attack, when you feel low, when there is no evidence of any change, feelings and emotions can start to rise that are aimed at taking your focus off where you are going, off your goal and onto your current situation or even your past. When this happens you must be quick to act and work at the following exercise until the negative emotions have passed. Think of emotions and feelings as a wave. When it comes in it hits you, but it will pass. You must simply stand your ground and prevent the emotions from leading you into old negative behaviour and speaking patterns. The following exercise will interrupt this emotional cycle; it is like having a personal version of Deuteronomy 28. And, once completed, it will not only help you to break old negative patterns, it will create a positive force of motivation which will enable you to press on through the difficult moments that we all experience in the process of renewal.

Action

Start a new page in your journal and at the top of the page write down the words "Joy", "Pleasure" and "Blessings" as a heading. Now read through each goal one at a time and ask yourself, "When this goal is completed what will it mean to me, what joy, what pleasure and what blessings are going to be in my life immediately, mid term and long term?" When you have an answer, ask, "What else?" And just as in the goal setting process, keep asking this question over and over until you have exhausted all the answers.

Now, on a new page write the words "Pain" and "Destruction" as a heading. Read through your goal again and ask yourself, "If I do not persevere to make the change and see this goal completed, what is it going to cost me? What pain and destruction will come into, or continue in, my life right now, mid term and long term?" When you have an answer, ask, "What else?" And just as in the goal setting process, keep asking this question over and over until you have exhausted all the answers.

Let your writing be expressive; this is the time to use emotion. In both instances multiply what it is going to cost you spiritually, emotionally, financially, physically etc. Now keep this list with you and read it whenever you have a dark moment or day. Remind yourself of who you are according to the Word of God and where you are going and why.

So many times we act without being aware of the consequences. As I look back on my life, if I had been consciously aware of the pain and destruction that I was going to cause and reap, both for myself and others, through some of the decisions that I made and the actions that I took, I would not have made the mistakes I have made. This little exercise could save you a lifetime of pain through making you aware of the consequences of taking a particular action. You can use it anytime you have a big decision to make.

Having a black and white factual account of why you want to achieve your goals also helps create the excitement and adrenalin that will push you on to keep going that extra mile. Most successful entrepreneurs have this ability to drive forward when many others would have given up. It is because they are focused on the reasons why they are taking action, and what they are going to receive at the end. God created us to be motivated to receive a blessing.

Purposeful days result in a purposeful life

"Give us day by day our daily bread.
And [day by day] forgive us our sins,
For we also [day by day] forgive everyone who is indebted to us.

And do not lead us into temptation,
But [day by day] *deliver us from the evil one."*   (Luke 11:3–4)

The secret of your success is determined by what you focus on each and every day of your life. Living every single day with purpose compounds, and one day you will see the cumulative effect of living each day at a time with focus and purpose.

Once you have identified the vision God has for your life, set your goals and created an action plan, and once you have identified negative beliefs and are working on renewing your mind with the truth of the Word of God, the secret of your success then lies in living each day with the Holy Spirit and with purpose. Jesus commands us not to worry about tomorrow:

> *"Therefore do not worry about tomorrow, for tomorrow will worry about its own things. Sufficient for the day is its own trouble."*
> (Matthew 6:34)

He taught us the importance of keeping the focus in the moment. It is what you say and do today that will either build up or tear down your life.

We were created to live daily and this is why Jesus taught us to pray for daily bread, not weekly or monthly bread; He taught us that it is daily dependence upon Him, daily walking with Him, daily forgiveness, daily protection, daily deliverance that brings us peace. This is the where the Lord's prayer leads us. There is something very powerful about only having to work on issues for the day. It is contrary to the world, it is an activity of the Kingdom of God and it is liberating. Try it!

Action

Pray and commit this exercise to the Lord. Ask yourself, "How do I want to live today?" Write down your answer in the following way:

- **Today** I will trust You explicitly
- **Today** I will live by Your Word
- **Today** I will walk in the light of the vision You have given me
- **Today** I will remain 100% positive in everything I say
- **Today** I will speak words of life in every circumstance that I find myself in
- **Today** I will walk in love, forgiveness and tenderness
- **Today** I will deny myself and be a servant
- **Today** I will care for my body, watching carefully what I eat and drink

Now ask the Lord, "What do You want for me today, Lord?" Here are some of the answers He gave me:

- **Today** stay close to Me
- **Today** listen to My voice
- **Today** let Me lead you
- **Today** know that I love you and am working out My purposes for you

Continue to turn your answers into a list of statements about how you want to live today and then live like this *every* day keeping your focus just in the day you are living.

> "Yesterday is gone, tomorrow is a promise,
> today is a gift which is why it is called the present!"

Planning your day

> *"Most assuredly, I say to you, the Son can do nothing of Himself, but what He sees the Father do; for whatever He does, the Son also does in like manner."* (John 5:19)

The Holy Spirit has a plan for your day! It is not a random erratic plan, it is a carefully thought out plan. Jesus only did what He saw the Father doing; He lived by revelation knowledge. He is our model; He worked in perfect partnership with the Holy Spirit. In the book of Acts we see over and over the Holy Spirit leading the disciples, instructing them, warning them; He wants to do exactly the same for you.

Ask the Lord to reveal His daily plan for you. Commit to Him your daily tasks and plan with Him. Prayerfully use the following questions to help build a framework for each day. Write up your answers to these questions each night or at the beginning of each day so that you wake up and hit the ground running with an outline from the Lord.

At the close of the day ask the Holy Spirit

- What is Your specific focus for me tomorrow?
- What do You want to accomplish in me tomorrow?
- What do I need to do and when will I do it?
- Who do You want me to contact/see tomorrow? Who is on my mind and why? (Pray)
- Is there anything You want me to put an end to/finish tomorrow?
- What do You want me to begin tomorrow?
- What was great about today?
- What did I learn today?
- Who am I grateful for right now? How can I show them?
- What is wonderful in my life right now? (Thank and praise the Lord)
- Am I trusting, am I positive and speaking Your language?
- Am I expectant for You to do great things for me and through me tomorrow?

At the beginning of the day

- Read through your vision statement, your goals and speak out your proclamations and affirmations.
- Read all the "just for today" statements about yourself.
- Read all the answers from last night.
- Pray. Commit your day to the Lord. Ask the Holy Spirit to empower you, fill you. You need Him, He is your Helper, He wants to Help you today.

You are now in a very different position from when you started reading this book; life is not going to be the same because you now have knowledge and skills that if practised daily will bring you the manifestation of the victory of the Lord Jesus in every situation in your life. Whenever you feel yourself drifting, go back to the plan. Daily stay diligent in prayer, daily read the Word, and daily read your goals, daily practise your affirmations and proclamations and you *will* see deliverance. The Word of God never returns void, never!

The Spiritual Warfare of the Mind

The teachings you have received in this book were specifically designed to enable four things to happen. Firstly, for you to learn about your mind and how the enemy works through your thought life. Secondly, for you to learn how the Lord Jesus Christ is formed in you and lives in you by the Spirit through the renewing of your mind. Thirdly, to teach you how to identify and pull down strongholds in your mind that are contrary to the Word of God and be delivered from demonic oppression. Fourthly, for you to learn how to discover the will and the purpose of God for your life and to begin to walk in His calling.

If you have put into practice the principles you have learned you will by now be back up on your feet, you will have identified the work of the enemy in your thought life and you will be working with the Holy Spirit to put off the old belief system and build new beliefs according to the Word of God. The presence of the Lord Jesus will be increasing daily in your life as you are being transformed through His ever-increasing presence in your mind. Having done all this there is now one more step for you to take in order to stand in victory against the devil; you must pick up and use the spiritual weapons of warfare that you have been given as a believer in the Lord Jesus.

Ephesians 6:10–18 reveals to us exactly what these weapons of warfare are and why, how and for what purpose we must use them. Child of God, you are involved in a battle, a battle to enforce the victory of the Lord Jesus in your life. There are two opposing forces, the Spirit of God in you and heaven's armies, and the god of this world, who is the devil with his forces of fallen angels and demons. And there is an objective, for you to stand in the victory of the Lord against the devil's schemes and to overcome all his attacks on your life.

Everyone who believes in the Lord Jesus is involved. We are all engaged in spiritual warfare. It is not something that a select group of believers do; no, we must all appropriate the victory of the Lord Jesus in our lives by individually using the authority we have in Him to pull down strongholds and overcome the works of the devil. No one can do this for you, because the battleground is in your mind.

Your purpose in this battle is to stand, and having done everything, to remain standing. Your job is to maintain your position in the Lord because the enemy wants to steal it. He wants to take ground from you; he wants to regain the authority and control he had in your life before you believed, but it is through your faith that the Lord will undo the works of the devil. Your faith destroys him, and this is why Satan's attack is always aimed at your mind, because it is out of your mind that faith, belief and trust in God operates, and it is through you that the Holy Spirit flows to perform the will of the Father on earth today.

Beloved, if you have fallen know this: when you fall you do lose ground to the enemy, but the moment you turn back to the Lord, the second you repent and fully set your mind to obey the Word again, you are restored, you are forgiven, the blood of Jesus cleanses you from all unrighteousness and in the Lord you can now put back on the *full* armour of God and reclaim your rightful position again. Child of God, there is now no condemnation; it is time to renew your mind and re-engage in the battle.

"Finally, be strong in the Lord and in his mighty power. Put on the full armour of God so that you can take your stand against the devil's schemes. For our struggle is not against flesh and blood, but against the rulers, against the authorities, against the powers of this dark world and against the spiritual forces of evil in the heavenly realms. Therefore put on the full armour of God, so that when the day of evil comes, you may be able to stand your ground, and after you have done everything, to stand.

Stand firm then with the belt of truth buckled around your waist, with the breastplate of righteousness in place, and with your feet fitted with the readiness that comes from the gospel of peace. In addition to all this, take up the shield of faith, with which you can extinguish all the flaming arrows of the evil one. Take the helmet of salvation and the sword of the Spirit, which is the word of God. And pray in the Spirit on all occasions with all kinds of prayers and requests. With this in mind, be alert and always keep on praying for all the saints."   (Ephesians 6:10–18 NIV)

This passage begins with a command, to be strong in the Lord and in His mighty power. We do this by putting on what is termed "the full armour of God". The full armour of God is in fact a belief system; it is a mindset in total harmony with the Spirit and the Word of God. The armour of God is a mind that has been renewed with the knowledge of God and has therefore established a key set of core beliefs founded on the Word of God. The Holy Spirit is the creator of these beliefs, because they are formed by the Word of God.

This mental armour is essential in order to be able to stand in the battle against the enemy. With this armour in place the mighty power of the Lord can be released through you to destroy the schemes of the devil in your life and ministry. The armour Paul is about to describe to us consists of seven specific components, which are seven core beliefs that must be in place 24/7 in order for you to be prepared for and able to withstand the attacks that will come during your life on earth. These attacks are identified as coming from one source only, not flesh and blood, but a spiritual being, who Paul names as the devil. The Greek word translated "devil" in this text is *diabolos*. It is another name for Satan which is used to reveal to us a certain aspect of his character; it means "accuser" or "slanderer" and it originates from his accusation and slander of God in the Garden of Eden.

The devil has an army of fallen spiritual beings. These are the third of the angels of heaven who fell with Satan, and he is their commander-in-chief. These fallen angels are described by Paul as rulers, authorities and spiritual forces of evil in the heavenly realms, and it is they who execute the devil's schemes and assignments against believers and lead the rest of mankind astray and away from God. The rulers (*arche*) are high-ranking spiritual beings in positions of authority. The authorities (*exousia*) describe spiritual beings who not only have the physical capability to act but the authority to execute that action. The powers (*kosmokrator*: *kosmos*, meaning "world"; *krateo*, meaning "to hold") are fallen angels who are world rulers who operate under the direct instruction and authority of Satan. And finally we read of spiritual forces of evil; the Greek word for evil in this text is *poneros* meaning "sorrow, labour, pain, wickedness, maliciousness and evil". The forces we struggle with are high-ranking spiritual beings who have the ability and authority to rule over mankind. This authority comes directly from Satan who became the god of this world through the fall of Adam.

Note that they are spiritual forces of *poneros*. They are the forces that are behind the sorrow, labour, pain, wickedness, maliciousness and evil in the world and they were also given their places of spiritual authority by Satan through the fall of Adam. The curse that was pronounced in the Garden of Eden was one that brought *poneros* to mankind because through the fall man became subject to the direct rule and authority of Satan and his fallen angels. It is only by being born again through faith and the freewill choice to follow the Lord Jesus that a person comes out from under this demonic rule as they are transferred into the Kingdom of God.

> *"For he has rescued us from the dominion of darkness and brought us into the kingdom of the Son he loves."*   (Colossians 1:13 NIV)

However, through sin and unbelief the enemy can gain a foothold in a believer's life and once this has happened repentance and renewal of the mind is required on our part in order for the Lord to evict the enemy and restore us to our position of authority in Him.

Jesus referred directly to Satan as the *poneros* one, the evil one, and in John 17 He asks His Father twice to protect, watch and guard the disciples; in verse 15 He makes it clear who they need this protection from: *"My prayer is not that you take them out of the world but that you protect them from the evil one* [the *poneros* one]*"* (NIV). When the disciples asked Jesus to teach them how to pray, He taught them to make this same request: *"Our Father in heaven . . . lead us not into temptation, but deliver us from the evil one* [the *poneros* one]*"* (Matthew 6:9, 13 NIV).

It is against the *poneros* one, the evil one, Satan and his fallen angels who are the rulers, powers and authorities of this world that we must take our stand. Jesus has given us complete authority over all the power of the enemy (Luke 10:19–20). But we need to learn how to exercise and enforce the Lord's authority.

In light of the understanding of whom we struggle against, in Ephesians 6:13 Paul commands us for the second time to put on the *full* armour of God in order to be able to stand when the day of evil, the day of *poneros* comes. This usage of the word *poneros* to relate to the evil day reveals to us that it is the devil and his forces that are behind the attacks and times of trial in our lives. The Greek word for "day" is *hermera*, and it means "a full twenty-four hour period" or "any part of that day". The devil has schemes, which in the Greek is *methodeia*, and refers to a methodical, technical, orderly manner of procedure. Child of God, the devil has a methodical, detailed thought-out strategy and plan to pull you down. The enemy has set days when he performs these carefully thought-out assignments against us. It is not random, but carefully planned and strategically executed. When these hours, days and times come upon us it is too late to act then; we must be prepared beforehand and we do this by putting on the full armour of God which a belief system that is formed by the Holy Spirit through the renewing of your mind with the Word of God.

The first piece of the armour is the belt of truth. Truth (*aletheia*) is the inner mental knowledge and belief in the One who is the truth, the Lord Jesus who is the Word of God, and the subsequent decision to speak, walk and live only in His truth. Jesus described Satan as the father of lies and therefore all who lie are speaking on behalf or under the influence of Satan.

> *"You are of your father the devil, and the desires of your father you want to do. He was a murderer from the beginning, and does not stand in the truth, because there is no truth in him. When he speaks a lie, he speaks from his own resources, for he is a liar and the father of it."*   (John 8:44)

Satan's work is specifically aimed to divide your mind and he will attempt to do this by lying to you and by enticing you to speak lies yourself. Lying is in fact the ultimate evidence and fruit of a divided mind and therefore the starting point and the first line of defence and protection is for us to renew our minds with the truth, by being filled with the Spirit of truth.

> *"However, when He, the Spirit of truth has come, He will guide you into all truth."* (John 16:13)

The breastplate of righteousness (*dikaiosyne*) is the second piece of armour and is put in place after the belt of truth. It represents the full belief of sole reliance in the righteousness of the Lord Jesus which is accredited to us by faith and not by our own works. It is our total trust and unquestionable belief in what the Word of God says about righteousness, that we have none of our own and that we depend only and solely on the righteousness of Jesus and that through Him we are justified in God's sight. Beloved, this belief is *the* answer to the condemnation of the devil who is the accuser of the brethren. It is described as the breastplate because it is the guardian and keeper of your *kardia*, your heart, your subconscious and the belief system that it contains. The conscious and sure knowledge that you are washed in the blood of the Lamb guards your life when you take your stand against the accuser, and it is *the* belief that will silence the inner lie and voice of condemnation that is sent to destroy your faith.

The third piece of armour is *"feet fitted with the readiness that comes from the gospel of peace"*. Readiness is an attitude; it is an active state of mind as opposed to a lazy unbelieving attitude to faith. If we truly believe in the Gospel and the words of Jesus we have to be ready for action, prepared in advance for what is coming.

> *"Therefore keep watch, because you do not know on what day your Lord will come ... So you must also be ready, because the Son of Man will come at an hour when you do not expect him."*
> (Matthew 24:42, 44 NIV)

In this and many other parables Jesus warned us against the perils of having a lazy attitude, because a lazy attitude is one of unbelief. We must be ready, mentally prepared, aware, informed, expectant, and sharp against the wiles of the enemy. No good soldier is caught sleeping by his enemy, for he also comes and attacks at a time when we least expect him.

The fourth piece of armour is the shield of faith and it follows the attitude of readiness. What do you do with a shield? You lift it up when a sword or an arrow comes against you; and this is exactly how you use the shield of faith in your mind. You activate your belief in the Word of God and let faith rise up to protect you in your thinking against every thought that comes to set itself up against the knowledge of God. Using the shield of faith requires believing and speaking out the living Word of God in every situation in your life.

According to this scripture, faith is a shield that has the power to extinguish and bring to nothing every single attack of the enemy; it puts out *all* the flaming arrows of the *poneros* one, the evil one, not one or two arrows, all the flaming arrows. Your faith safeguards your life *"who are kept by the power of God through faith for salvation"* (1 Peter 1:5).

True faith operates through a mind that is renewed and fully believing in the Word of God. Total trust and belief in the Lord will bring to nothing *all* the carefully planned evil strategies of the rulers, authorities, powers and spiritual forces of evil. Isn't that wonderful? Your faith, child of God, is more powerful than the power of the demonic world rulers. Your faith is greater that the devil, because the Lord works through your belief in Him. It is He who extinguishes all the flaming arrows as you put your trust Him. This is why the enemy attacks your mind, because it is through your mind that the power of God works to destroy the devil and his works.

Take the helmet of salvation and the sword of the Spirit which is the Word of God. The helmet, the Spirit and the sword are grouped together and are the last but one of the seven pieces of the armour of God. The Greek word for "take" is *dechomai* and it means "to readily accept and receive as a gift". The helmet of salvation is the knowledge of God, which comes through the Spirit of God and the Word of God. It is the reliance upon the truth of the gospel that you are saved, forgiven, washed, redeemed, restored, deeply loved, that there is hope for your future and that you are called for a purpose.

The Word of God in this text is the *rhema* word, the spoken, living, God-breathed Word of God. It is the specific word, given to you by the Spirit at a specific time, in a specific situation for a specific purpose. It is different from the *logos*, the written and whole revelation of God's Word. The *rhema* word is a personal word direct from the Father that the Holy Spirit delivers to you. It is a revelation of the will of the Father for your life that the Spirit brings. It is not the wisdom of this world but the wisdom of your heavenly Father and this wisdom will instantly transform your belief system the moment you receive and believe it. It is through your belief in the *rhema* word, that the word becomes the Holy Spirit's sword against the devil and He uses it to create life, to create breakthrough, to bring to pass the will of the Father, and to defend you and destroy the works of the enemy.

The final piece of the armour is the spoken word. The language for this battle is prayer in the Spirit. Prayer in the Spirit is an act of faith and is the outward manifestation of a mind that believes the answers lie with the Lord. Prayer in the Spirit is the evidence of a mind that is subjected to the Spirit, dependent on the Spirit and trusts in the Spirit and is in love with the Spirit, because it is out of the heart, the mind, that the mouth speaks, and prayer flows out of our mouths according to the beliefs we hold within.

Child of God, putting on the armour is another term for putting on the new man, which is putting on the Lord Jesus. You will win the battles in your life through having a mind that is absolutely set on Him and totally believing in His Word. This is how you do it, because this mindset is one of faith and trust that releases the power and authority of the Lord Jesus in you. This is how you exercise your authority over the devil on earth, through unwavering faith and belief in the Lord, His cross, His death, His resurrection and His Word. With the full armour of God, that is every one of these fundamental beliefs firmly in place, you will experience victory over the forces described in this text, and the power and might of the Lord will be released in your life to execute the victory of Jesus.

This, beloved, is actually the fulfilment of the greatest commandment, to love the Lord your God with all your heart, with all your soul, with all your mind and with all your strength. May you grow to love Him in this way and in so doing experience the awesome, extraordinary, victorious, abundant, overflowing life that Jesus has won for you.

Conclusion

In closing I would like to share with you one of my deepest personal experiences of the power carried in our words. My mother was a beautiful, dynamic, amazing woman and yet, apart from brief moments in her life, she lived in fear and in a negatively-charged environment. Her self-talk, the words she heard and received into her mind, her belief system, was unknowingly and invisibly working to destroy her life.

On 24th April, 2003, I spent the morning with my mother, and for the first time in my life I saw her in bed not feeling well. The doctor was called and she was given the all clear, but she was not "all clear", she was dying. At 8 p.m. that evening she phoned me to say that she was finding it difficult to breathe and that another doctor had visited and called for an ambulance. It took over an hour and a half for the ambulance to arrive and by the time she reached the hospital every organ in her body was systematically closing down. Finally, at 10 p.m. her heart stopped beating. Minutes later I received a telephone call from my brother to tell me that my mother had died and the cause of death was unknown. At two o'clock in the afternoon my mother and I were together and by ten o'clock that night she had died and no one knew why. The doctors could not diagnose the cause of death. The post-mortem discovered that she had bone marrow cancer.

In Hebrews 4:12 we read that the Word of God is sharper than any two-edged sword dividing between soul and spirit, joint and marrow. This scripture teaches us about the location of the spirit. Your spirit sits inside your mind, and is guarded and protected by it. In the same way your bone marrow sits inside your bones and is protected by them. Your bone marrow produces white blood cells which fight infection, red blood cells which carry oxygen and nutrients around the body, and platelets which enable blood clotting and healing. In the same way your spirit was designed by God to receive life from Him and to release His protection, nourishment and healing to your mind and therefore into your body and your life.

However, just like a bone, your mind can become broken (Luke 4:18) and in my mother's death I see a picture of a mind that had been so utterly broken down over time by the evil power contained in the destructive words that ran through her mind that eventually her spirit too became crushed. And according to the Word of God a broken spirit results in the lack of the will to live. In the same way any disease, breakdown or failure of the bone marrow will ultimately result in physical death.

> *"A happy heart makes the face cheerful,*
>   *but heartache crushes the spirit."*   (Proverbs 15:13 NIV)

> *"A man's spirit sustains him in sickness,*
>   *but a crushed spirit who can bear?"*   (Proverbs 18:14 NIV)

The very part of her that should have been receiving life from God and nourishing her whole mind and body became shattered. The real cause of her death was a crushed spirit that was caused by the destructive force at work in the negative and evil words that she allowed herself to believe. Her subconscious had received those words as fact and in turn had released poison into her body which ultimately manifested itself physically as bone marrow cancer.

If I had known then what I know now, I could have helped my mother to identify and resist Satan's attack on her life; I could have taught her how to resist him, renew her mind, to become strong and live victorious in the Lord. Who knows, she might still be alive today. The Lord, however, has spoken to me through her death and through the lives of the people that He brings to me for coaching, and He has shown me the awesome reality of the power that is released through our words and the wonderful way that His Spirit works in our minds. Being born again through faith in Jesus is like having a bone marrow transplant. The life-giving Spirit of God comes to dwell in your mind and release His protection, deliverance, healing and nourishment into every area of your mind, body and life, if you let Him through the renewing of your mind.

Child of God, what I have shared with you in this book can change the course of your life. My prayer is that you will now lay hold of the truth and apply it to your personal life and the situations you face and so experience the Son of God living through you in a way that will cause you to experience true joy, true hope and true life in all its fullness.

About the Author

In 1996 Lesley founded a Christian ministry called 'The Branch', leading small groups to Jerusalem and the deserts of Israel and Jordan, staying in remote areas to pray and learn about God in intense and challenging situations. But in the year 2000 her own life fell into a crisis.

It was in the midst of this intense time of extreme personal difficulties and challenges that Lesley received a revelation that was to change the course of her life forever. Through hours of study and prayer the Spirit of God revealed that her life could be completely transformed through the renewing of her mind, a process that required positive action on her part. In 2003 Lesley started studying for a diploma in Life Coaching, qualifying with distinction with a thesis on the Biblical Principles of Life Coaching and she immediately started to see the lives of those she coached radically transformed through the power of God at work in the principles she taught.

In 2005 Lesley felt a strong call to start writing and to capture in a book the revelation and understanding she had received about renewing the mind and the mind of Christ. Today Lesley is ministering biblical coaching both corporately and privately to many individuals whose lives are in despair and without hope. There are testimonies of people who have been saved from depression, suicidal despair, failed marriages, the grip of pornography and many desperate situations. Lives are being turned around within days through the power of God at work in the coaching process, and people are experiencing dramatic healing of both body and mind.

The vision and call on Lesley's life is to enable people to be set free from the situations that are destroying their lives. She has known great darkness and failure in her own life but also knows through personal experience that there is no situation, no circumstance or problem that cannot be solved by Jesus Christ if you continue to hold on to Him for life. She knows His deep desire to set people free and to bring His healing and restoration to their lives. And, she has received a revelation of **how** to bring His healing to people through the renewing of their minds.

Her passion now is to reach as many people as possible through her book and the medium of television and radio with a message of hope and the promise of the amazing and purposeful life that is available to everyone through faith and trust in Jesus Christ.

www.lesleymalpas.com

We hope you enjoyed reading this New Wine book.
For details of other New Wine books
and a range of 2,000 titles from other
Word and Spirit publishers visit our website:
www.newwineministries.co.uk
email: newwine@xalt.co.uk